A

MEASURE

OF

SUCCESS

A

MEASURE

OF

SUCCESS

From Assignment to Assessment
in English Language Arts

Fran Claggett

Boynton/Cook Publishers
HEINEMANN
Portsmouth, NH

Boynton/Cook Publishers
A subsidiary of Reed Elsevier Inc.
361 Hanover Street
Portsmouth, NH 03801-3912

Offices and agents throughout the world

"On Marking the Mind of a Student" by Fran Claggett originally appeared in *Black Birds and Other Birds, Poems 1951–1976* by Mary Frances Claggett, Taurean Horn Press, 1980.
Credits continue on page 216

Claggett, Mary Francis.
    A measure of success: from assignment to assessment in English language arts/Mary Frances Claggett.
        p.   cm,
    Includes bibliographical references and index.
    ISBN 0-86709-373-0
    1. Language arts—United States—Ability testing.   2. English language—Composition and exercises—United States—Ability testing.   3. Reading—United States—Ability testing.   I. Title.
LB1576.C558   1996   95-33583
372.6'044'0973—dc20   CIP

Editor: Peter Stillman

Printed in the United States of America on acid-free paper
98 97   DA   2 3 4 5 6

For Madge Holland, a constant measure of success

On Marking the Mind of a Student

by Fran Claggett

Reading your paper   I am struck
   again
         (or still, for I am always
         reading your paper)
             by the
   what can I call it
           by the pure shaft
  of mind   splitting
        thought   into its known
        (but not to be proved)   smallest particles
reversing the assumption that
            fission
       is a disintegrating process.

Your words   set down upon the line
  (in ink, on one side only please,
      and watch the margins)
  shimmer randomly   and
                  bounce
       against the whiteness
         of the page
  there
     no
          there
(How can I read them when they won't
      stand still)   indicating their presence only
  by their movement
         by their
  ever–shifting dance
       upon the lines
(now wavy to my eyes from trying
  to follow the optical illusions
     of your mind).

Dance, logos, dance upon the page
  my red pen (felt-tipped, irrevocably)
     suspended
        above you, not able
    to violate the poetry
      of your prose
    descending only once
         to inscribe
  in that signal, ineffective way
    the mark of one mind
      upon another.

Contents

Acknowledgments

I wish to acknowledge the students and teachers who have taught me the value of focusing on success—in teaching, in learning, in assessing. A special thanks to the students whose work appears in these pages. Foremost among the teachers I want to acknowledge are the members of the California Assessment Development Team, a group of outstanding classroom teachers, kindergarten through university, with whom I worked for three days every month for a period of ten years designing, developing, and scoring various levels of reading and writing assessment programs. Particular mention must go to Charles Cooper, Professor Emeritus of the University of California at San Diego, whose ideas about writing gave shape to the writing assessment design, and to others who served as consultants during different stages in its process: Mary Barr, Director of the Center for Language in Learning; Mel Grubb, Consultant in Language Arts for Los Angeles County; and Sheridan Blau, Professor of English at the University of California Santa Barbara. Key team members in articulating the theoretical basis for the integrated reading and writing assessment were Terry Underwood, Elk Grove School District, and Lynda Chittenden, Mill Valley Schools. Lynda also willingly wrote up one of her inimitable solutions to assessing fourth graders in the section "Report Cards: A Burning Issue." Martha Dudley, from Selma, and Nancy Preston, from Torrance, kept me in touch with the realities of middle school students. Beth Breneman, Barbara Weiss, Jill Wilson, and Juanita Jorgensen from the Department of Education provided invaluable logistical support and leadership. Special mention, too, to Educational Testing Service consultant Barbara Voltmer for passing along her expertise in conducting impeccable scoring sessions; and to Sherry Arnold, Amy Barr, Linda Murai, Darby Williams, and other staff members at the Sacramento County Office of Education for their invaluable work with the assessment project.

To Joan Brown and Kelly Smith, whose work appears as separate chapters in this book, I extend my gratitude for their willingness to share their experience and expertise as teachers extraordinaire. Joan also provided both insight and feedback on early chapters and on the continually changing organizational structure of the book. Ruth Vinz, from Columbia University, and Louann Reid, from the University of Colorado, my co-authors on other Heinemann-Boynton/Cook texts, contributed to the evolution of the "angles of vision" delineated in Chapter Four.

No acknowledgments would be complete without mentioning the work of those researchers and thinkers whose work has so powerfully affected my thinking about teaching, learning, and assessing. Of most immediate relevance to this book are Louise M. Rosenblatt, for her seminal work with aesthetic and efferent purposes in reading and writing; Judith Langer, for her work with the concept of envisionment, stances, and horizons; Alan C. Purves, for his ideas about *difficulty* in literature; and Elliott Eisner, for his inspiring work on the role of the arts in cognition.

Finally, I want to thank Peter Stillman, great friend as well as discerning editor, for his patience, support, and insightful editing. On any rubric for editors, he ranks at the top.

Introduction

Taking Our Measure

We need to move from metaphors that are technocratic to ones that are humane, from those focusing on the mechanical to those that embrace the organic, from the literal to the imaginative, from the depersonalized to that which is more personal, to pay attention to productive idiosyncrasy instead of being preoccupied with standardization, and to pay more attention to the structure-seeking and less to the rule-abiding. Only a totalitarian society wants a cookie-cutter model of educational outcomes. We should want something more for our children.
Elliot Eisner, Stanford University
NCTE Address, 1991

"Look,"cried Chicken Little, "the sky is falling!" "Look," cry the educational watchdogs, "standards are falling!" All around us, people are talking about *standards*. The government wants national standards. Business leaders demand graduation standards that will tell them whether applicants for jobs can read and write. Parents want to know how their children measure up. Realtors from California to New York point to state test scores when they are pushing sales of houses in "good school" areas. Students begin cramming for the SAT in the eighth grade; they've learned early that colleges take their measure from test results.

Dominating the education news in the public press and fed by the business community is the issue of graduation or exit standards—

external measures that would hold students accountable for mastery of learning, however variously *learning* is defined. What is less obvious from both the public press and professional journals is that the national resurgence of attention to standards rides on the wave of teacher reform of a different sort at the classroom level. While politicians and business leaders form commissions, allot moneys, and discuss policy, teachers, long dissatisfied with the mechanistic, standardized approach to assessment, are experimenting, conducting research, participating in dialogues, attending conferences, and developing models for a humane, personal kind of assessment that acknowledges different learning styles, different cultures, different ways of perceiving the world. It is teachers who, recognizing the interrelationship of curriculum and assessment, are challenging the use of uncontextualized multiple-choice tests at district and state levels. *Standards* has emerged as the educational metaphor of the decade. Whether it becomes mired in the technocratic bubbles of the multiple-choice advocates or flies grandly as the banner of the authentic assessment reformers is up to the only group that can truly implement any policy, local or national—classroom teachers.

Changes in the teaching and assessing of writing began in the mid-1970s with the inception of the Bay Area Writing Project (the seed group for what has become the National Writing Project). With the nucleus of a network, English Language Arts teachers moved beyond their own classrooms to expand their understanding of how assessment could encompass a range of processes involved in students' writing. As teachers looked at writing as a springboard to all learning, they also began to look critically at other aspects of student performance—reading, collaborative work, graphics, presentations. The networking facilitated by the writing project sites that grew up all over the country provided strong impetus for teachers to address what had long been a major concern: that the assessment of a student's performance in reading and writing cannot be contained in a single numerical or letter grade. This concern, evident in other disciplines as well—mathematics, science, history/social science, vocational education—has led to serious experimentation with alternative measures of assessment, notably the many versions of performance-based assessment that are coming into use. The visual arts, of course, have long depended on portfolios to assess a student's achievement; it is a natural extension of using performance to assess achievement.

Teachers are at the core of any meaningful reform in education, and both administrators and policy makers need to join with teachers in studying the complex question of classroom assessment as it both affects and reflects student learning. It is to these both practical and visionary teachers who, embracing "the organic, from the literal to the imaginative," in Eisner's words, are exploring authentic, curriculum-contextualized assessment at the classroom level, that this book is addressed, not with the prospect of easy answers, but with the hope of raising common concerns and exploring possibilities.

English teachers have always assumed responsibility for assessing the many threads that make up the fabric of student performance—achievement, ability, effort, and growth. Although school report cards traditionally exhibit a single letter or numerical grade for each grading period of the school year, there has traditionally been little agreement within a school or department about what that grade represented. Individual teachers themselves frequently change the balance between achievement and growth, ability and effort, depending on the nature of the class. Still, the convention has been to regard achievement as the primary factor, with ability, effort, and growth each assuming some proportion of importance relative to the individual teacher's philosophy or to the nature of the class.

Beginning with the school reform movement of the '90s, the unresolved debate about grading became subsumed under the umbrella of *standards*. For English teachers, however, the current concerns about assessment have deeper roots. Beginning in the mid-1970s, as Jimmy Britton's work with school writing in England began to influence large groups of teachers, primarily through the Bay Area Writing Project and its offshoots, teachers found that they had to rethink the entire process of marking student papers. Marking, the process of annotating and responding to a student's written work, became more clearly separated from grading, ascribing a single letter or numerical indication of student achievement. The long-simmering questions regarding grades as denoting achievement and/or ability, effort, and growth resurfaced as teachers paid more attention to the processes involved in writing, revising, editing, and responding.

The burgeoning interest in the holistic assessment of writing, which reached into classrooms throughout the country, spilled over into the assessment of reading. Most teachers had been accustomed to assigning a final paper or essay examination to determine student understanding of literature. Achievement in understanding or interpreting literature was too often dependent on student facility in writing the venerable, not to say hoary, five-paragraph essay. With the changes in the teaching of writing, however, teachers began to look more closely at the nature not only of writing, but also of reading, and at how we might better assess student understanding of literature.

The image of the stereotypical English teacher going home at the end of each day with an armload of papers and a supply of red marking pens has given way to a variety of assessment scenarios: the teacher and student in conference about the student's paper; the teacher audiotaping responses to student work; the teacher engaging in a written dialogue with the student about a project; the teacher or students videotaping a student project for later assessment by the students themselves; the teacher and student, along with parents, discussing the student's involvement in the various aspects of English while looking through an extensive folder or portfolio of the student's work. Although the letter grade is still a widespread culminating designation, the processes of *responding to* and *assessing* student performance have generally subsumed the more limited concepts of marking and grading. Teachers all over the United States are designing more inclusive approaches to teaching and assessing all aspects of student literacy. No longer does a student's facility in handling the written conventions of language dominate the teacher's perception of her or his ability to read and understand a story or poem. Thoughtful inquiry and research into the processes involved in reading have led to new ways of teaching and assessing.

Teachers employ both analytic and holistic approaches to assessment. With the increasing experience of teachers in the holistic scoring of large-scale writing and reading assessments, teachers have become skilled at incorporating these techniques into their classrooms, teaching students to become self-evaluators using personal as well as class-generated criteria. For particular assignments requiring close attention to specifics, analytic scoring is appropriate; here, too, however, teachers are helping students learn how to evaluate their own and each others' work. Providing guidance in peer evaluation as well as self-evaluation is a fundamental aspect of a teacher's inclusive approach toward assessment.

Evaluation of the multiple aspects of English Language Arts has always required attention to various kinds of classroom activities: reading, writing, speaking, and listening. Teachers observe students working alone and working on group projects; they pay attention to student approaches to problem solving and collaborative learning. Teachers regard student attentiveness, their propensity to listen and follow directions or to branch off on creative lines of their own devising. They observe students' ability to articulate their ideas to others, both in small groups and before the larger class audience. They take note of students' ability to conceptualize, as evidenced by student graphics as well as oral and written language. In all of these aspects of the continual assessment that teachers conduct, the constant activity is that of mindful observation.

The shift now is that teachers as a group rather than individually are focusing on how to incorporate their daily observations into an assessment system that is feasible, reliable, and understandable to all of the groups concerned about student achievement and progress. On a very practical level, teachers must devise methods of accounting for their assessment of student performance. The grade book, with its provisions for numbers or letters, is still a mainstay in the schools although teachers have long felt the limitations of the standard symbols that the typical grade book encourages by its very format. A student indoctrinated toward giving supreme importance to a letter grade may initially become impatient with alternative forms of written responses. "What did I get?" is a recognizable cliché. Teachers who have a wide repertoire of assessment strategies, however, teach students to assess their own work, often in peer groups or in consultation with the teacher. Alternatives to the simplistic, reductive report cards are becoming more commonplace as teachers incorporate learning records and portfolios into their total assessment of student work.

Teachers need to consider the appropriateness of their assessment practices for the various constituencies that they serve—students, parents, school administrators, colleges, or businesses—and the larger community—district, school, perhaps nation. While student growth over time might be germane to the student and parents, achievement according to a preset standard would be most relevant for comparing school and district scores. Some states have involved classroom teachers as primary designers of statewide assessment policies; indeed, teachers must be involved at the district and state levels of assessment if there is to be any meaningful impact of assessment on curriculum. Teachers who have participated in large-scale assessment development are only too happy to see their idiosyncratic marking systems give way to carefully benchmarked standards that will be meaningful to a broad audience.

As teachers cope with the complexities of the many issues that surround the daily classroom responsibility of assessing student performance, they utilize their own skills of reading, writing, speaking, and listening. The effective assessor is a careful reader of student work; an attentive observer of student participation in the various individual and group activities; a focused writer in responding to student papers. The cognizant teacher/assessor understands the value of rewarding what students do well and encouraging what they might improve; above all, the effective teacher models the art of self-assessment so that the many dimensions of assessment that are part of every class period become threads in the tapestry of learning that is taking shape for each student.

In the chapters that follow, I will take you into different classrooms to look at teachers' and students' own solutions to some of the issues central to the assessment of student performance in English classes and raise questions that still must be answered by individual teachers in their own classrooms. A later chapter will provide suggestions not only for individual teachers, but also for entire departments that are committed to improving the way they teach reading, writing, and thinking and will provide a model showing how one department's work, over a three-year period, resulted in an enhanced curriculum, more productive pedagogy, and authentic assessment practices. These are goals for all of us.

Reflections on a Grain of Sand

by Heather Fairbank
Coronado High School

Reflective essay written for the Grade 12 California Writing Assessment, 1988

> To see a World in a Grain of Sand
> And a Heaven in a Wild Flower
> Hold Infinity in the palm of your hand
> And Eternity in an hour....
> from "Auguries of Innocence"
> by William Blake

William Blake writes poetry about the insights gained from small things. Most of us are not skilled or creative enough to sum up our complex thoughts in four short lines. Often, even ten pages aren't enough space to express the revelations we derive from small occasions. At age seventeen, even after twelve years of schooling, it is difficult for us to articulate our thoughts on God, the world, or human nature. This is because our imaginations are taken from us during twelve years of practical education. Dreams and creativity are reserved for the very young and the "artistic" among us.

Perhaps we were all artists once, filled with dreamy imaginings based on the world around us, but those who remain artistic long find our society a difficult place. A good kickball player is appreciated more in grammar school than a young artist who fills his margins with doodles and creative scrawls. The ability to score well on a multiple choice test will get one farther in our school system than the ability to write good poetry. In our society, the deep insights gained from small things are gained at the expense of successes in a practical world.

Personally, the insights I've gained from small things tend to have a taste of guilt to them. Classroom windows can contain an incredible microcosm of American life, but the quadratic formula on the front chalkboard draws students away from it. Being on the inside, looking out, I've seen kids in the park playing, crying, and laughing. I've seen harried mothers trying to get two kids and a stroller across a busy street. I've seen volleyball players sweating in the hot sun, leaves twisting in the wind, and a slow rain splashing the cement. But these views that make me reflect are always ended by a squawk from the teacher, drawing my attention from the wonders of nature to the grammar we must be force-fed so as to be successful on all our multiple choice tests.

There has been a trend in architecture towards classrooms without windows. It is a big mistake. Without these glass squares, backroom dreamers and closet artists will miss the education that will serve them in later life. Small observations give our lives more meaning. The e. e. cummingses and William Blakes of the world will be remembered far longer than those who finished their math pages first. But how can these creative folks survive in a school system that emphasizes filling in the correct bubbles with number two pencils over the poetry one feels when staring out at a cloudless sky? I don't think they can.

A

MEASURE

OF

SUCCESS

Chapter One

Measure for Measure
Redefining the Subject

Est modus in rebus. *There is measure in all things.*
—Horace, *Satires*, Book 1

Teachers are engaged in assessment every minute they are in the classroom. As teachers, we are always observing, noting, and evaluating. Because assessment is completely integrated into the fabric of curriculum, our evaluations are just as accurate or as ill-conceived as the classroom experiences we design for our students. Before we even think about formulating or reconceptualizing our assessment philosophy, we must look carefully at how we view our subject, in this case the whole of what has come to be called English or English Language Arts. For simplicity's sake, I will use the term *English* to encompass the range of activities we are responsible for in English Language Arts.

In this chapter, I will deal with the ways we understand our subject matter, the theories about reading and writing that undergird our teaching and lead us to give particular kinds of assignments or design specific kinds of units. Whether we have articulated it or not, our personal philosophies about learning underscore every aspect of our teaching, determining not only the way we teach but also the way we evaluate student performance. By clarifying some of the assumptions we make about reading, writing, and thinking,

1

we can set up a framework for evaluating student performance in the various components that make up the dimensions of English.

Intelligence, as we have always supposed and are now coming to understand, is not a singular ability. During the rich brain-research period of the 1970s, our suppositions became grounded in the concepts of hemisphericity, and some of us designed our courses to appeal to both right-brain and left-brain ways of processing information.[1] During this period, too, American teachers became familiar with the work of Jimmy Britton, who gave us the terms *expressive, transactive,* and *poetic* to describe writing that serves different functions. We began to look more clearly at the purposes for which we use and teach writing. In the 1980s, Howard Gardner propounded his theory of multiple intelligences, delineating linguistic, musical, logical-mathematical, spatial, bodily kinesthetic, and personal intelligences. "In my view," Gardner writes in *Frames of Mind,* "if we are to encompass adequately the realm of human cognition, it is necessary to include a far wider and more universal set of competences than has ordinarily been considered. And it is necessary to remain open to the possibility that many—if not most—of these competences do not lend themselves to measurement by standard verbal methods, which rely heavily on a blend of logical and linguistic abilities." Later, Gardner calls for "the development of means of assessment that are fully adequate to the range of human skills which deserve to be probed."[2] The struggle to develop such "means of assessment" is the focus of this book.

The Four Functions

One of the difficulties we face as English teachers lies in the complexity of our subject matter; within our domain, we encompass most if not all of Gardner's "intelligences." How then can we assess student achievement and progress in the specific areas of our concern—primarily reading and writing? One way of folding assessment into our total approach to teaching is to look at ways of helping students develop the framework for becoming articulate, literate adults. By the time students reach our classes, whether we teach kindergarten, eighth grade, or seniors, they have developed strong predilections for the ways that they process information. In an effort to create a framework for reaching the dominant learning modes of all students, I have loosely translated Jung's concept of the four functions to make them applicable to teaching: The four functions are *observe, analyze, imagine,* and *feel* (Figure 1-1). By orchestrating umbrella assignments to encompass all four of these

Figure 1-1

Functions of the Four Functions

The four functions represent ways of making meaning of the texts
of our world through talking, listening, writing, reading:

Imagination	**draws us to vision**
Feeling	**grounds us in experience**
Observation	**connects us to our surroundings**
Analysis	**refines us through re-visioning**

functions, we can engage all students in their dominant learning
modes and help them extend their ability in the other functions.
Continual experience in all four functions will enable students to
develop what Gardner refers to as multiple intelligences and to become what Maslow calls a fully functioning human being. More
modestly, as English teachers, we can hope to help our students become thoughtful, critical, creative, literate adults.

"There is measure," as Horace wrote, "in all things." It is both
our joy and our challenge that language, the focus of our particular
subject matter, embraces the full range of the way human beings
speak, write, read, and communicate with each other. The complex
nature of our subject is further complicated by the fact that English
is both our subject matter and the vehicle for our study. As we continue to learn more about it, in all its variety and in all its dimensions, we must constantly redefine and refine the tasks we give our
students. Because reading and writing are the primary emphases of
the English curriculum, we need to look carefully at how we define
them; the way we view them determines how we approach both assignment and assessment.

A Definition of Reading

And no doubt that is what reading is: rewriting
the text of the work within the text of our lives.
—Roland Barthes

"Reading, writing, and arithmetic": easy words, words many of us
grew up with, if not "taught to the tune of a hickory stick," at least
taught in predictable, straightforward ways. *Reading* and *writing*

never needed to be defined. Like so much of childhood's easy knowledge, however, definitions of these concepts have become maelstroms of controversy, subject to multiple, oftentimes seemingly divergent meanings. As teachers, we are well along the way toward sorting out what we mean by writing, although it, too, moves in mysterious ways. Definitions of reading, however, are very much in the forefront of current literature of critics, theorists, and, most important for our immediate concerns, teachers.

Reading, as defined in much of the current literature, is a process of constructing meaning through transactions with text. In this view of reading, the individual reader assumes responsibility for producing an interpretation of a text guided not only by the language of the text but also by the associations, cultural experiences, and prior knowledge that the reader brings to the interpretive task. This view of reading emphasizes the role of the individual reader in making meaning through a process that brings together textual and contextual evidence and the distinctive experience and perspective of the reader as meaning-maker. It is a constructive activity in which, in Barthes' words, we rewrite "the text of the work within the text of our lives."

Aesthetic and Efferent Reading Purposes Defined

Louise Rosenblatt's definitions of aesthetic and efferent reading are central to understanding purpose in reading. Rosenblatt writes, "In aesthetic reading, the reader's primary concern is with what happens during the actual reading event. 'Listening to' himself, he synthesizes these elements (images or concepts or assertions that the words point to plus associations, feelings, attitudes, and ideas that these words and their referents arouse within him) into a meaningful structure."[3] When readers enter into an aesthetic reading situation, they bring their personal histories with them. They call on their past experiences and knowledge in order to make personal-textual connections. As readers actively engage in building a "text-world," they simultaneously enter and explore that world, thereby expanding their stores of personal memories. The recursive validation and expansion between text and self is central to the aesthetic reading process.

Rosenblatt writes that aesthetic readers weave "a web of feelings, sensations, images, ideas" between themselves and the text. As they weave this web, they become engrossed in the act of weaving as well as in reflecting on the web itself. They take risks, move into and out of the emerging web of meaning, bring ideas and feelings to the surface, then shape them into an interpretation that is, of course, always mutable in the light of further experience. "The distinction between aesthetic and nonaesthetic reading," Rosenblatt continues, "derives ultimately from what the reader does, the stance that he adopts and the activities he carries out in relation to the text. Implicit in this distinction . . . is recognition that the same text may be read either efferently or aesthetically."[4]

Although many texts might be read aesthetically, genres conventionally designed for this purpose include stories, novels, poems, essays, fairy tales, fables, myths, folk tales, and plays. Such texts invite personal discovery, growth, and change through the reading process. Since each reader transacts with the text to create his or her own web of meaning, interpretations of any given text necessarily vary. To be considered valid, however, a personal interpretation must be plausible given the evidence of the text and its contexts.

"In nonaesthetic reading," Rosenblatt continues, "the reader's attention is focused primarily on what will remain as the residue after the reading—the information to be acquired, the logical solution to a problem, the actions to be carried out. . . . To designate this type of reading, in which the primary concern of the reader is with what he will carry away from the reading, I have chosen the term *efferent,* derived from the Latin, *effere,* to carry away."[5]

Readers enter into an efferent reading event primarily to become more knowledgeable about a topic. In the most direct situation, readers expect to find out what happened or how a thing works; to gather data needed to complete a task or understand a process; to learn new ideas, concepts, and facts and perceive relationships among them. They may, however, go beyond the desire for pure information and read efferently to understand the writer's opinion on something—a restaurant, a book or movie, or an ethical or political issue.

When readers read efferently, they understand that their major work is to integrate new knowledge with their own existing knowledge; they come to these reading events to verify old knowledge with an eye toward refining, extending, or, in some cases, discarding it. Efferent readers establish and maintain a certain level of belief as they transact with the text, a level that is different from the requirements of aesthetic reading. Efferent readers expect accuracy from the text; they work to understand and organize the information in useful ways. Nonetheless, they also have the task of discovering the writer's perspective so that they can account for bias, distortion, even factual error.

As with the aesthetic stance, there are some text types that are commonly read primarily for an efferent purpose—factual materials, persuasive articles in magazines and newspapers, encyclopedia entries, and other traditional expository forms. It is important to note, however, that efferent reading events can involve narrative texts. The distinctions that are sometimes made between cognitive and affective responses as they concern narrative and expository texts do not apply here: both aesthetic and efferent reading includes cognitive and affective thinking.

Effective readers are actively involved in processes of reading. By bringing together the text, the context of the reading, and their own experiences, these readers connect with and challenge the text, deal effectively with uncertainty, and reflect on the meaning and implications of the reading.

How Writing Fits into the Aesthetic-Efferent Model

A model developed by a group of California teachers working on their statewide reading and writing assessment uses Rosenblatt's aesthetic-efferent framework to show how the reading and writing we do in the classroom fits into the broad concepts of purpose. Rather than denoting only the two extremes, this model depicts four categories of purpose, applicable to both reading and writing.

Readers and writers have related yet different purposes within each of the four reading and writing events that encompass the spectrum from aesthetic to efferent: to shape and have aesthetic experiences; to express one's own experiences and connect with another's; to influence or persuade and to evaluate another's point of view; and to understand and convey information. Table 1-1 shows basic reader and writer purposes. As you look at the table, remember that these are not intended to be pure categories; rather they denote primary emphasis on the part of the reader or writer. Nearly all reading and writing events are composed of a mix of purposes.

The focus of the relationship between the reader or writer and the text varies, depending on the category: In the aesthetic experience, the focus is determined by the text itself—its form, its language; in the expressive category, focus is on the writer; in the persuasive category, focus is on the reader; while in the efferent/informative quartile, focus is on the subject matter of the text.

The dominant reader and writer purposes listed in the table for each category become secondary purposes for each of the other events. These purposes can be simple, mundane, and singular; however, they can also be extremely subtle, complex, and mixed to the degree that speaking of *one* purpose for a particular act may distort the intention. Nonetheless, it is reasonable to speak of dominant

Table 1-1

Purpose Category	Reader Purpose	Writer Purpose
Aesthetic	To live through an aesthethic experience; To connect to universalities of experience	To give shape to an ideas or an experience, real or fictional
Expressive	To connect with another's personal experiences or ideas	To create, reveal, or clarify ideas or experiences for self or other
Persuasive	To consider and evaluate another's point of view	To influence or convince another of one's ideas or judgments
Efferent/ Informative	To understand information; To gain new knowledge	To convey information; To explain ideas, facts, or processes

purpose as we think about the assignments we make and how we assess them. Placed in the context of the four functions, reader and writer purposes may be synthesized as follows:

- Aesthetically, we *imagine*, experience, shape language and ideas.
- Expressively, we *feel,* recreate our experiences, connect with others.
- Persuasively, we *analyze*, consider, convince.
- Efferently, we *observe*, record, convey our information to others.

If we are aware of how purpose shapes our language, we will be more conscious of the kinds of assignments we make and the criteria by which we assess them. We will be conscious, too, of setting our goals toward having students select their own purposes. Since most of us like to do what we do well, we can assume that our students, as they learn and internalize strategies for fulfilling our diverse purposes, will become not only more effective but also more active readers and writers. We may look toward adults who keep their own journals, buy books, and use the public libraries.

Chapter Two

Assigning and Assessing Reading

About Reading . . .

Now and then there are readings that make the hairs on the neck, the nonexistent pelt, stand on end and tremble, when every word burns and shines hard and clear and infinite and exact, like stones of fire, like points of stars in the dark—readings when the knowledge that we shall know the writing differently or better or satisfactorily, runs ahead of any capacity to say what we know, or how. In these readings, a sense that the text has appeared to be wholly new, never before seen, is followed, almost immediately, by the sense that it was always there, that we the readers, knew it was always there, and have always known it was as it was, though we have now for the first time recognised, become fully cognisant of, our knowledge.

—from *Possession* by A. S. Byatt

In her novel *Possession*, A. S. Byatt describes the kind of reading that I hope has happened to every reader of this book, the kind of reading that I think most of us hope for our students to experience, preferably while they are in one of our classes! Can it be taught, this kind of reading? How can we know when it happens? How can we help it happen? And, if we are so fortunate as to acknowledge that this kind of reading experience has happened to a student during our tutelage, do we, or *how* do we assess this student's epiphany?

After reading an excerpt from Richard Wright's *Black Boy* in which Wright discovers the power of books, a student, taking a state-wide reading assessment, responded at one point like this: "His (Wright's) reaction to the books he read was that of any normal human being at first, but then he started taking books much too seriously. He started to realize that books bring you much knowledge, so he then began the craving for them. But his craving for books and knowledge got the best of him, they snatched him from reality as if he were going to heaven. Each book he read seemed to become a part of him in such a way that they set his mood until he was finished." Clarence Williams, in grade ten at Ramona High School in Riverside, California, has something in common with A. S. Byatt, esoteric British novelist. They both use images of heaven (or the heavens, as in "points of stars in the dark") as they separately describe an event that transcends most of our everyday reading experiences. Whether Clarence Williams has experienced the kind of reading that transported Wright, we do not know; we do know that, in reading the words of *Black Boy*, he was able to bring his own understanding of reading to bear on his interpretation as he articulated Wright's experience.

To create an opportunity for students to do just that—articulate their interpretations—calls for some teaching that may differ dramatically from the way many teachers have traditionally assigned and assessed the reading of literature. The kinds of questions we frame, the kinds of group projects we pose, the kinds of papers we assign—these are the topics we must address in order to be able to help students become *transactive* readers. They are the same topics we must explore if we are to become effective assessors of our students' achievements in reading and, even more to the point, if we are to help our students become close observers of their own achievement and growth as readers.

Framing the Literary Reading Experience

Ideally, we want all students to come into our classrooms as avid readers. These students were probably, but not always, read to when they were children. As teenagers, they frequent the library, take out armloads of books, and read. We don't have to think about motivation. We don't have to dream up ways of enticing or threatening them into a book. Ideally, too, we as teachers have time to read something other than student papers! But this is the real world. Some of our students do love to read. Others not only don't like to read, they are just beginning to learn to read English. Some of them enter our classrooms nearly illiterate in any language.

At this point, I am going to assume that you have an extensive individualized reading program in place. Here I want to address the reading that you have students do in common. Most departments now have specific novels and plays required for all students at a particular grade level. Rarely, I notice, do departments have short stories or poetry on their required reading lists even though these genres pose the greatest rewards for the actual teaching of reading strategies. (Read on if you are about to take offense at the possibility that I might be talking about *dissecting* poems. I object to dissection even in the high school biology laboratory!)

First question: How much do you tell students about a work before they read it? This is not an easy question. Motivation is a critical issue. On one hand, you want to have students think about what they already know about the subject or nature of the work or author before they read. On the other hand, the nature of literature is that it is designed to activate these experiences during the reading. To say too much dulls the experience. It's like going to see a movie that you have heard all about from an enthusiastic friend. Some teachers design extensive prereading exercises, from having students write on the subject that is the theme of the work to giving them elaborate outlines of what they will be reading. Let me point out the danger of the extensive prereading approach: Whatever prereading exercise you design will have been filtered through *your own interpretation* of the work. As a result of working on the design, fieldtesting, and implementation of a statewide reading and writing assessment, our team of teachers discovered that at first we were unconsciously building into the prereading questions our own conclusions about the meaning of the story or poem we were asking the students to read. Such questions dramatically limited and proscribed the interpretations students posited. Suggestion: Rethink the ways that you motivate students to begin reading a particular work. Be aware of your own interpretation and bias toward a work and try to keep it out of your early discussions with the class. There will be time later to share your ideas about the text.

Making the Process Visible

How do you help students actually read a text? What strategies will be useful during the process of reading to elicit the transactive processes that promote the engagement of minds—of reader and writer? The most critical foundation of any reading strategy at this level (beyond decoding) is to make the process visible to the reader. One of the seminal characteristics of the learning process itself is that during learning we pay attention to what we are doing. We focus on the steps that later become so habitual we have trouble sorting them out from the larger activity or behavior. In the classroom, even at the upper grade levels, where we assume students "know how to read," we need to spend some time helping students focus on the act of reading itself. As with so many aspects of teaching and learning, it is important to balance metacognitive activities with those that focus on end results, such as reading for the pleasure of the story alone.

Annotating a Text

Some people seem to be born annotators. Others are reluctant to stop the process of reading long enough to write down their thoughts as they read. I suggest that we should teach all students how to annotate as they read, then let them find their own predilections once they know the process. Certainly a student's reading ability should not be assessed on the basis of whether there are margin notes; but such notes, when present, should be taken into account, as I will demonstrate later in this chapter. To teach the process, begin with a short work—a poem, an essay, or a short story. Photocopy the work, leaving a wide margin on the right or wide margins on both sides. Distribute copies of the work and ask students to write down whatever thoughts they have about the work as they read. Frame this exercise as just that, an exercise, like practicing scales or shooting baskets. After the students have read, have them discuss, in small groups, the nature of their responses—not the meaning of the work, but the kinds of responses that they made. Then, as a whole class, list the kinds of responses they made. They will probably fall into such categories as these:

- rephrasing or paraphrasing what they think a word, line, or section means
- identifying with something in the work: "That is like a time when I . . . ."
- stating confusion or uncertainty as to meaning: "I don't understand . . . ."
- indicating total frustration or boredom: "This is stupid."
- arguing with the author: "Who says so?"

- agreeing with the author: "This is absolutely right!"
- speaking directly to the author, perhaps to express appreciation ("I love the way this sentence sounds.") or to question the need for something in the story ("Why did you have to make her do that?")

Responding to the Whole Work

Before discussing the work, either in small groups or as a class, students should have an opportunity to formulate their initial ideas about it. By having all students engage in this activity individually, the reluctant or shy students are assured of having some ideas or opinions about the work when they do get into group discussion. The important thing to convey to students here is that this is an *initial* response, not a final one. Students who tend to make up their minds early and stay with their first ideas about a work are cutting themselves off from the benefits of others' ideas as well as of their own reflectiveness. Keeping in mind the definition of *reading* as the *construction of meaning*, teachers might well spend some time with students pointing up the value of an interpretation over time, a reflective interpretation that takes into account various views, different ways of looking at the elements of the work, and ideas that are continually being re-considered, extended, and perhaps revised. As students become more adept readers, they will, of course, see such benefits themselves and come to value their own ideas as well as possible interpretations advanced by other students. Experienced readers will also understand how to incorporate the views of their teachers and published critics without allowing these views to lessen the importance of their own.

The nature of the activities and questions that enable students to extend and deepen their understanding must come from the particular text that students are reading. Because reading is a process rather than a static activity, there is no set formula for designing such questions and activities. There are, however, some general kinds of questions and activities that have proved to be productive in taking students more deeply into a work. The activities suggested here are intentionally open: each can be adapted to relate to particular classes or groups of students as well as to the individual work that is the focus for the reading. These questions and activities are designed to help students move beyond their initial response to a deeper exploration of meaning of the specific work they have read. They both invite and direct students—individually and in small groups—to demonstrate their reading of a literary text by

- connecting the text to their own experience, e.g., to incidents they have experienced or observed, other literature, works of art or other media
- taking risks as they experiment with multiple possibilities of meaning and as they make and revise evaluations
- transacting with the text, forming and reforming opinions, making assumptions, drawing inferences
- reflecting, alluding to the text, questioning it, quoting from it, rethinking their first response to it, refining their understanding

Suggested kinds of questions and activities:

- response logs
- dialectical or double-entry journals
- charts and diagrams pointing up various kinds of comparisons
- graphics (sketches, maps, symbolic drawings) with follow-up explanations
- predictions
- speculations, as in directions to write a new ending, draw a missing scene, and so on. (Be sure, when using speculative questions, that they are tied specifically to the text.)
- close study of textual elements, as
    - characters, ideas, images, symbols
    - one character's changes during the text
    - the impact of setting on character behavior
    - the reader's reflection about what s/he thinks after reading and working with the text; e.g., "What I first thought . . . What I think now,"accompanied by an "account for the change" component
- connections to other literature and other art forms
- open-ended questions eliciting interpretation, reflection, evaluation, speculation, and so on
- evaluations of textual elements such as language, form, and so forth

As a kind of parallel to the unstructured initial response question, there should also be an unstructured final opportunity for students to express any insights, issues, or concerns that developed during the reading process, responses that might not have been elicited by other activities. Students may, through their writing or drawing on this page, come to closure and/or discover new insights emerging from their reading experience. Even though this response has a sense of being a final interpretation, since it may conclude one phase of a reading experience, it should be looked on as final in the sense of "for the time being" or "at this point in my thinking." Students should begin to see that their interpretation of a work of complexity and richness may continue to change. To emphasize this possibility, departments might reprise certain provocative works as students progress through their schooling. The comment from a junior that "Oh, we read that in eighth grade" should be met with, "I know! And now that you are older and more insightful, you will see it in an entirely new way!"

Reading a Text for Persuasive or Informational Reasons

The reading of texts for persuasive or informational rather than aesthetic or literary purposes proceeds along much the same lines as those just outlined. Although any text can, of course, be read efferently, there are some slight shifts of emphasis that I will mention here.

In some situations, students may need to access prior knowledge and current opinions about an issue before they become engaged with the author's argument. The prereading activities should be judiciously prepared so that students are not led into an interpretation or a position but are invited to record the knowledge and opinions they bring to the subject. This activity sets up a later question of whether or how their ideas have changed as a result of the reading. Note that this extensive use of prereading activities contrasts with the use of prereading strategies in preparing students to read for aesthetic purposes.

Annotating and the initial response are as useful in reading persuasive and informational articles as they are in reading literary texts. The questions that follow fall into the same categories as well; the difference lies in how those activities are selected for the particular aspects of an efferent text. Generally, such questions here will focus on the following kinds of thinking:

- *restating* in a purposeful way
- *relating* information from the text to prior knowledge and/or personal experience
- *analyzing* through comparison and contrast, drawing inferences and asking questions
- *evaluating*—accepting or rejecting the writer's judgment; or giving evidence that they have considered all sides of an issue.
- *extending* ideas, making predictions, speculating, showing how information may apply to their own lives
- *reflecting*, considering the effects of the information or arguments in a text on their own position or attitudes

Assessing the Student's Literary Palate

At the beginning of a term, it is useful for both students and teachers to have a sense of what kind of reading the students have done, what kind of books they enjoy, and how they see themselves as readers. Following is a suggested way of carrying out this initial self-assessment. It is addressed to the student.

What Kind of Reader Are You?
A Self-Assessment

"We are what we eat," we are told. But we are also what we do, what we think, what we read. Part of growing up is developing your own taste—in food, in clothes, in music; one's taste is important because it reveals something about who we are. This process involves cultivating what people in the food business call "an educated palate," a wide-ranging knowledge of and appreciation for different kinds of foods. Educating your literary palate as well as your food palate is partly what this class is about. In this survey you'll explore ways of describing your literary palate at this point in your life. Read the following comments and see which ones come closest to describing you:

- Anorexic Reader ("I can't even pick up a book.")
- Perpetual Diet Reader ("I read only what I am assigned; I'd like to read some other things, but I have to stay on my diet to pass my courses.")
- Fast Food Reader ("I read *Cliff Notes* and the summaries at the ends of chapters. I never have time to sit down to a whole book.")
- Omnivorous Reader ("I'll read anything and everything. I read newspapers and magazines and books and cereal boxes, comics and billboards. I read T-shirts. I have been known to sit at a fast food counter and read the label on a ketchup bottle.")
- Trendy Reader ("I read only what's in. If it isn't being talked about by my friends, I don't bother.")
- Vegetarian Reader ("I read only nutritious articles and books. I want what I read to nourish me spiritually. I wouldn't think of reading books that had been made from animals.")
- Gourmet Reader ("I'm very selective about what I read. I know what makes good literature and I read only the best.")

Discussion: You may have found that you have qualities of more than one kind of reader. Share your perceptions of your literary palate with your group. Then talk about the following ideas and questions:

- Try to describe your early memories of learning to read—whether you liked to read, hated it, found it easy or hard.
- Share some of the books you remember from your early days as a reader.
- Talk about when you're most likely to read—in the summer, during the school year; at night? What is the last book you read? What kinds of books do you generally read? Do you have a favorite book or author?
- What are your goals for yourself in reading? Do you want to be able to read better? Faster? Why? Mostly for practical reasons—to make studying easier? To survive in your career? Or mostly for pleasure, enrichment?

After you have finished your discussion, write a journal entry on the subject of "You Are What You Read." Write a description of how your reading reflects who you are. How does your literary palate provide clues to who you are as a person? Give your entry a title, to help you remember the focus of it and put the date at the top.

Alfred, Lord Tennyson, writing about Ulysses on his return from his ten years of traveling from Troy to Ithaca, had Ulysses say, "I am a part of all that I have met." In the same way, you can say that you are a part of all that you have read. As you expand your literary palate in this class, you'll meet other people through their writing; each encounter will add something not only to the kind of reader you are, but to the kind of person you are.

Structuring a Balanced Reading Program

With all of your insights into the reading habits of your students, and all of your knowledge about the nature of reading, structuring a comprehensive reading/literature program may seem daunting. The questions of breadth and depth persist. The questions about how much time to allot to individual in-class reading time and outside reading need to be answered for each class, each year. These questions, however, must be considered as you plan how to assign, teach, and assess your students' growth and achievement in reading. As indicated earlier, I subscribe to a curriculum that includes extensive student choice in reading. I also believe that we owe it to our students to teach poems, stories, essays, plays, and novels of high literary merit. This is not the book in which to deal with such critical issues as canon, non-canon, multicultural literature, and feminist literature. It is the place, however, to introduce the question of what kinds of reading to include in a reading program because it is that balance that determines how a student's reading growth or achievement will be evaluated. In my view, an effective reading program includes emphasis on two strands: one, extensive reading of books and other texts selected by the students; and two, works selected primarily for their literary merit and taught by the teacher. Student-selected books might be completely open choice or limited by specific curricular goals such as the study of a particular genre, of a period of history (especially in team-taught courses), or of an issue that is the focus of a unit of study.

The question of student accountability for books read to encourage fluency, to develop a habit of reading, or to augment the core reading of the class is one that arises frequently. The old-model book report is still widely used although most teachers have found ways to make such reading more integral to the class. Students want and need feedback on their reading. One way to structure both self-assessment and teacher assessment of student-selected reading is through the use of the *reading record*. Using this plan, students, during a typical nine-week period, record their reading either daily or weekly, depending on how you structure it. The reading record might take several forms; a simple one, a 5" × 7" card, appears as Figure 2-1.

Figure 2-1

The Reading Record

Name				Class, Period	
Date	Title	Author	Category (sci fi, e.g.)	Pages/ Time	Comments

Throughout the marking period, students engage in book discussions within groups. Before assigning such discussions, it is helpful to have a model "fishbowl" type of discussion, perhaps about a story everyone has read. The teacher and a few students form a group and have a short discussion, observed by the rest of the class. During subsequent discussions, teachers can, from time to time, listen in, participate, make suggestions, and generally monitor the discussion. At other times, the teacher can arrange very brief but useful individual conferences. Teachers might ask students to tell about the books they are currently reading or discuss their overall reading. Questions emerge naturally from the book cards.

At the end of the marking period, students tally up the number of pages they have read. They then write an evaluation of their reading for the quarter based on such questions as those that follow. You may wish to specify certain questions that all students respond to while leaving others to student choice. Another possibility is to list all the questions and have students write an evaluation in which they select those areas that are most meaningful to them. This list is intended to be suggestive only, not definitive:

- Look at the books that you read this quarter. If there were any that you did not finish, tell why you didn't finish them. (This is not a judgment; there can be many reasons why we don't finish books.)
- Look at the categories you read this quarter. Were you reading mostly in one category? In several? Did you read in any category new for you this year? What do you like most about book in the categories that you read? What new category might you try next quarter?
- What was your favorite book this quarter? Tell what you liked about it.
- What was the most difficult book you read this quarter? What was difficult about it? How was it worth or not worth the difficulty of reading it?
- Tell a little about how you selected the books you read this quarter. Were any recommended by friends? By your parents? By your teachers? By the librarian? Did you just see a book on the shelf and think it looked good? Did you read any books because of seeing the movie on which it was based?
- About how much time did you spend reading each week? When do you find time to read? Do you wish you had time to read more or are you reading as much as you want to now?
- Write a short summary evaluation of your reading for this quarter. Base your evaluation on the time you have spent, the amount you read, your interest in the books you have read, and the quality of the books you selected.

With the use of reading records, there is always the question of whether the student actually read all of the books listed. I have found that by monitoring group discussions and having individual conferences about the books, I have a fairly clear idea of who has read what. In addition to these methods, however, I mark one book on each student's reading record and ask the student to write specifically about it. This part of the assignment might read something like this:

I have marked one book on your book card. For this book, you may do one of the following activities:

1. Create a graphic showing the main theme of the book. Include quotations that you think are interesting and important in conveying this theme.
2. Create a sun-shadow mandala for the main character of the book. Write a short character sketch or poem after you finish the mandala. (See Appendix One)
3. Write a review of this book for the school newspaper.
4. Prepare a short book talk for the class, telling them why you recommend or do not recommend this book for them to read.

The reading records and accompanying papers or projects become part of the student's portfolio of work for the quarter (see Chapter six for a full discussion of the classroom portfolio). If you work on the basis of individual points or grades, you can assign points for student-selected reading based on several criteria: number of pages read, quality of books read, and student self-evaluation.

Whatever structure you set up for the management of your reading program, it is important not to lose sight of the overriding goal of instilling a deep love of reading, of literature. We try to enable students to read fluently, to interact with the story as they read, to make good choices that stretch their imaginations and extend their understanding of the full range of human experience. How we know whether we are achieving this goal depends on how well we read our students.

Vanessa Granillo, a grade 7 student at El Sausal Middle School in Salinas, California, was writing in her journal one day when I was visiting her class. Her teacher had asked his students to respond to the question, "Why do we study literature?" I asked Vanessa if I could read what she wrote. What I read was this:

> We study literature (which is something you read, a story, poem or play) to assist us in understanding our own personal selves, other human beings or our human nature *and* to assist us in understanding the so-called "real world" *and*, most important, to set goals.

> We study literature to travel to different places, to experience new things, to escape from the harsh realities of the real world and to assist us in conflict resolving.
>
> We study literature by transforming or becoming part of the story. By using or exploring our unlimited source of imagination and by experiencing new ideas, feelings, emotions, dreams, goals, passions, hopes, adventures, conflicts and thoughts through the character.

The first two paragraphs sound like a conscientious student telling the teacher what she has heard, what she has been taught; the third paragraph, however, uses the material in the first two paragraphs to say something important about the writer's own experience. This statement comes from reading, from "becoming part of the story." The ability to articulate this understanding makes it more powerful for this writer. I am interested in the idea that Vanessa states twice, that we study literature "to set goals." I would like to ask Vanessa what she means by this. What literature has helped her to set what goals?

Reading Vanessa's journal gives her teacher insight into Vanessa's ideas about the value of literature. Her journal entry, along with all the other indications of her reading—her choices of books, her range of interest reflected by her reading record, her dialectical journals accompanying class reading— contribute to her teacher's overall assessment of Vanessa's reading performance.

A Rubric for Assessing Achievement in Reading

Evaluating achievement in the *process* of reading is quite another matter. For many teachers, this evaluation has been based solely on a test or essay that the student wrote following study of a literary work. That method, while possibly a good evaluation of the student's essay-writing skills, does not address the quality of a student's reading. For a meaningful assessment of reading achievement, I strongly recommend using a rubric or scoring guide. The following scoring guide was designed by a group of teachers who worked over a period of some years developing an integrated reading and writing assessment for use in California. It evolved through many drafts based on results of extensive fieldtesting and close analysis of literally thousands of student responses. Since its development, many classroom teachers have found it extremely useful, although it was originally designed for a large-scale assessment. The introduction and list of reading performances have been slightly adapted for classroom use. Some teachers prefer to teach the scoring guide to their students early in the school year. The most successful use, however, follows the process of having students create a scoring guide themselves after they have learned a number of reading strategies and experienced what it means to be a transactive reader. When they are given the following scoring guide (or some version of it), students will be pleased to discover that the one they created is very closely aligned with it. It always happens. Once understood, the scoring guide can be applied both as a means of student self-evaluation and as a teacher tool for assessing student reading achievement.

Introduction to the Reading Scoring Guide

Reading, as defined for the purposes of this book, is the process of constructing meaning through transactions with text. In this view of reading, the individual reader assumes responsibility for producing an interpretation of a text guided not only by the language of the text but also by the associations, cultural experiences, and knowledge that the reader brings to the interpretive task. Rather than believing that meaning resides solely within the words on the page, this view of reading emphasizes the role of the individual reader in making a meaning through a process that brings together textual and contextual evidence and the distinctive experience and perspective of the reader as meaning-maker.

To assess a student's performance in reading is therefore to assess not only the richness and plausibility of the meaning that the student produces but also the quality of the process through which meaning is produced. A score should be based on an interpretation that is supported by plausible reasons and/or references to the text, even though the student interpretation may differ from the scorer's interpretation.

While we assume that every effort has been made to construct reading activities that give students multiple opportunities to demonstrate their ability to construct meaning from interacting with given texts, it is important to emphasize that each individual reading score represents the reading achievement of a particular student, on a specific day, reading a given text. It is also assumed that any specific reading score will be considered in the context of the student's total portfolio. Complex factors that affect student responses include the purpose of the reading, as established by the reading activity and perhaps modified by the student's own purposes; the nature of the reading questions and activities; and the student's previous experience with the text type or with the subject of the text.

Reading Performances

Effective readers demonstrate a range of reading behaviors, at least several in depth. Through their talking, writing, and graphics, these readers show convincing evidence of their ability to construct meaning. Even insightful and discerning readers do not necessarily show evidence of all the performances listed below in any one reading. Such readers, however,will usually display a broad spectrum of reading behaviors or a few selected behaviors in great depth. The exemplary reader generally shows variety, complexity, breadth, and/or depth. The performances that characterize effective reading include these: The reader will

1. demonstrate intellectual engagement with the text: experiment with ideas; think divergently; take risks; express opinions; speculate, hypothesize, visualize characters or scenes, explore alternative scenarios; raise questions; make predictions; think metaphorically
2. explore multiple possibilities of meaning; consider cultural and/or psychological nuances and complexities in the text
3. fill in gaps; use clues and evidence in the passage to draw conclusions; make warranted and plausible interpretations of ideas, facts, concepts, and/or arguments
4. recognize and deal with ambiguities in the text
5. revise, reshape and/or deepen early interpretations
6. evaluate; examine the degree of fit between the author's ideas or information and the reader's prior knowledge or experience
7. challenge and reflect critically on the text by agreeing or disagreeing, arguing, endorsing, questioning, and/or wondering
8. demonstrate understanding of the work as a whole
9. attend to the structure of the text: show how the parts work together; how characters and/or other elements of the work are related and change
10. show aesthetic appreciation of the text; consider linguistic and structural complexities
11. allude to and/or retell specific passages to validate and expand ideas
12. make connections between the text and their own ideas, experience, and knowledge

13. demonstrate emotional engagement with the text
14. reflect on the meaning(s) of the text, including larger or more universal significances; express a new understanding or insight

Scoring Guide Descriptors

Score Point 6: Exemplary Reading Performance

An exemplary reading performance is insightful, discerning, and perceptive as the reader constructs and reflects on meaning in a text. Readers at this level are sensitive to linguistic, structural, cultural, and psychological nuances and complexities. They fill in gaps in a text, making warranted and responsible assumptions about unstated causes or motivations, or drawing meaning from subtle cues. They differentiate between literal and figurative meanings. They recognize real or seeming contradictions, exploring possibilities for their resolution or tolerating ambiguities. They demonstrate their understanding of the whole work as well as an awareness of how the parts work together to create the whole.

Readers achieving score point 6 develop connections with and among texts. They connect their understanding of the text not only to their own ideas, experience, and knowledge, but also to their history as participants in a culture or larger community, often making connections to other texts or other works of art. Exceptional readers draw on evidence from the text to generate, validate, expand, and reflect on their own ideas.

These readers take risks. They entertain challenging ideas and explore multiple possibilities of meaning as they read, grounding these meanings in their acute perceptions of textual and cultural complexities. They often revise their understanding of a text as they reread and as additional information or insight becomes available to them. They sometimes articulate a newly developed level of understanding.

Readers performing at level 6 challenge the text. They carry on a dialogue with the writer, raising questions, taking exception, agreeing or disagreeing, appreciating or criticizing text features. They sometimes suggest ways of rewriting the text. They may test the validity of the author's ideas or information by considering the authority of the author and the nature and quality of evidence presented. They may speculate about the ideology or cultural or historical biases that seem to inform a text, sometimes recognizing and embracing and sometimes resisting the position that a text seems to construct for its reader.

Score Point 5: Discerning Reading Performance

A reading performance at score point 5 is discerning, thorough, and perceptive, but will probably show somewhat less insight or sensitivity to nuances and complexities of text than an exemplary reading. These readers are able to fill in gaps in a text, making plausible assumptions from subtle cues; but they engage in these operations with less acuteness of vision than do more expert readers. They recognize and differentiate between literal and figurative meanings. They recognize real or seeming contradictions, exploring possibilities for their resolution or tolerating ambiguities. They demonstrate their understanding of the whole work as well as an awareness of how the parts work together to create the whole.

Readers achieving score point 5 see connections between their own lives and the world of the text. They connect their understanding of the text not only to their own ideas, experience, and knowledge, but also to their history as participants in a culture or community. They often make connections to other texts or other works of art; these connections, while always purposeful and connected to the text, may be more predictable than those made by exceptional readers. They also draw on evidence from the text to generate, validate, expand, and reflect on their own ideas.

These readers may explore multiple possibilities of meaning. While they may form firm interpretations early in their reading, they are open to revising their ideas as additional information or insight becomes available to them. They sometimes articulate newly developed levels of understanding.

Readers performing at this level challenge the text. They pose questions, postulate answers, take exception, agree, disagree, and speculate; however, the questions and/or issues they raise may not be as insightful or perceptive as those of the reader demonstrating an exemplary reading.

Score Point 4: Thoughtful Reading Performance

Readers at score point 4 construct a thoughtful and plausible interpretation of a text. They fill in some gaps in a text, making assumptions about unstated causes or motivations, for example, or drawing meaning from cues in the text. They usually differentiate between literal and figurative meanings. They may recognize real or seeming contradictions, but are sometimes distracted by these contradictions and by ambiguities. They demonstrate their understanding of the whole work.

Readers achieving score point 4 develop connections with and among texts. They usually connect their understanding of the text to their own experience and knowledge, and sometimes to other texts. When directed, these readers may generate, validate, expand, and/or reflect on their ideas about the text, but with less depth than in a 5 or 6 response. These readers tend to paraphrase or retell, often thoroughly and purposefully. They also see, however, a more general significance in or wider application of the literal facts of the text.

These readers, while confident, rarely take risks. They accept the text without exploring multiple possibilities of meaning. They tend to present their understanding of a text as fixed and rarely revise their interpretation as they reread and as additional information becomes available.

Readers demonstrating this level of reading performance sometimes challenge or question the text. They may raise questions and may agree or disagree without explaining their reactions.

Score Point 3: Literal Reading Performance

Students performing at score point 3 are literal readers, constructing a plausible but superficial interpretation of the whole work. They show little sensitivity to nuances and complexities; they may not respond to some portion of the text. They usually demonstrate a grasp of the whole work, but at a simplistic and literal level.

These readers develop few or no connections with or among texts. Sometimes they connect the text associationally with personal experience, but the connection is generally superficial and unexamined.

Score point 3 readers are not risk takers. They show little tolerance for textual difficulties or lack of closure. Confronted by textual complexity, they are inclined to ignore the difficulties. Their reading process tends not to be recursive: having made some initial sense of the text, they are inclined to retain their view without testing or revising it.

Readers at level 3 rarely challenge the text or carry on a dialogue with the writer. If they raise questions at all, the questions will be largely unproductive expressions of frustration or low-level inquiries (i.e., about word meanings). Any expressed appreciations or criticisms are likely to be simplistic and based on a literal understanding of the text.

Score Point 2: Limited Reading Performance

A limited reading performance indicates that readers at score point 2 construct partial and/or reductive meanings for a text. They may demonstrate a superficial understanding of parts of the text. They demonstrate a reductive meaning for the text by overgeneralizing or oversimplifying, but seem unable to grasp the whole.

Readers within this range of performance develop few or no connections with texts. They may, as they recognize some idea, continue to write or draw, but their responses will appear to have only a tangential relevance to the text.

These readers seldom ask questions of a text or offer meaningful evaluations of what they read. They tend to abandon or become entangled in difficult sections of a text.

Score Point 1: Minimal Reading Performance
In a minimal reading performance, the reader appears to understand and respond only to an individual word, title, and/or phrase, but not in ways that demonstrate even a rudimentary understanding of how these words relate to text ideas.

Any connections such readers may make to their own experience will appear in the form of words or drawings that have textual associations only to an isolated word or phrase. Minimal responses may include vague and unsupported evaluations or responses (e.g., "I like/don't like this story," or "It's boring.") Level-1 reader responses suggest that these students do not engage in reading as a process of making coherent meaning.

Applying the Rubric: The Teacher as Mindful Observer

In the day-to-day observations that constitute a teacher's most direct methods of assessment, the list of reading performances can be invaluable. Although the language in this list is geared toward the older student, it can easily be adapted for use with younger children. The performances themselves, however, span all age groups. The teachers who worked to develop this list originally thought that they would end up with very different reading performances for, say, fourth graders and sophomores. Not so. Fourth graders demonstrated every performance listed, although not, of course, in the same balance or with the same degree of insight. Before using this (or any other) list of performances, it is important to validate it by finding examples of the performances in student behavior and work at the grade level you teach. Whether you use the performances in this guide or generate your own list, it is important that you and your students are thoroughly familiar with the behaviors that mark effective reading. Students can be taught to monitor their own reading behaviors, noting which performances they consistently use and which they rarely do. By helping students focus on their own reading processes, you can tailor your instruction—individually, in groups, or with the whole class—to helping students increase the effectiveness and broaden the range of strategies they bring to the reading process.

The questions and activities listed earlier as being particularly useful in engaging students in the processes of reading allow both students and teachers to note and evaluate the uses of specific reading performances. Two of these, the response logs and the dialectical or double-entry journal, are elaborated here as basic strategies underlying a sound reading program.

Response Logs

Rather than moving directly from a reading experience into analysis and interpretation, it is important to allow the power of the piece of literature to work its magic. Suppose you have just read a poem to the entire class. Students have their own copies and may or may not have read along. A common classroom procedure is to jump right into discussion, throwing out questions such as "What is this poem about?" You can almost predict which students will immediately have an opinion and express it, perhaps even eloquently. A common scenario would show a good discussion following, but it would probably be limited to the teacher and from three to five students engaging in an analysis of the poem. What is going on in the minds of the rest of the students who have heard and read this poem? Perhaps one is agreeing with the ideas of a vocal student. Perhaps another is confused, wondering how they got such an idea. Another may be thinking about the game after school. Another might be doodling, half listening.

Here is another take on this poem. You read a poem aloud to the class. Before the reading, you remind students to have their response logs out. After the reading, before any comment about the poem by anyone, even the teacher, students write or draw their initial response. If a question is needed at this point, try something like, "What do you make of it?" Note the subtle difference from the earlier question "What is this poem about?" That question can come later, if it is needed. After writing their initial responses, students get into small discussion groups and share their ideas. Note that all students will now have something to say. They may read their logs or talk about their sketches. They may comment on each other's ideas. Even if some students remain quiet during this period, they will have ideas in their minds. As they gain confidence, most students will eventually look forward to this kind of exchange. After a brief period, perhaps only ten minutes, you call the whole class back together for a large-group sharing of views. Divergence of opinion is encouraged (see #1 on the list of reading performances). This is the time when you introduce your own take on the poem. By this time, students have enough assurance in their own ideas that they can listen to your interpretation without immediately, unquestioningly accepting it. At the point when the discussion is still vibrant but waning a bit, ask the students to return to their logs and respond reflectively, using questions such as "What do you think about this poem now? How does what you think now tie into what you wrote earlier? If your ideas have changed, explain what changed them." After such an exercise, students are ready to move into a deeper analysis of the poem, if that is indicated, or go on to the next part of the day's work. Perhaps you read the poem as a way of leading into the reading of a novel. In this case, a further discussion of the poem would wait until after they had read the novel.

Responding to Students' Response Logs

How do you assess such an exercise? There are two fertile areas for assessment here: One is observation of the small group discussions and the other is in the second half of the log, the section in which the student describes a change in ideas and attempts to account for the change. Once students have become accustomed to this process, they have a lot to say. You will find many examples of the reading performances showing up in their logs. You can be specific in eliciting particular performances, such as asking students to refer to specific parts of the text to explain their ideas (no. 11 on the list). The most important thing about this strategy is that it allows the poem or story to do what it is intended to do—inculcate ideas and feelings in the readers as they bring their own experiences to create their own interpretations of the text.

Teacher comments are always at the heart of the teacher-student relationship that develops as you give students your insights into their ability to read and make sense of their reading. Comments may be as brief as a word as you walk around the room talking with students individually or as formal as responses to "final" papers. In between are the written comments that teachers make as they read response logs. Following are two examples of student responses with teacher comments. At this stage, the teacher is building confidence, commenting in a conversational way to the students' ideas.

Reading Response to "The Democratic Order: Such Things in Twenty Years I Understood" by Alice Walker

Ignorance

by Jason Cheng, Grade 12: Teacher, Joan Brown

Student Response

Teacher Comments

The little girl in the poem was beaten. It wasn't her fault though. It wasn't her father's fault either. It was the fault of ignorance which leads to hatred. It was the fault of those evil men in the white hoods. It was the fault of the white man who yells 'nigger.' It was the fault of a half a century of families separated, brothers whipped, mothers crying, senseless dying.

When the father of the young girl comes home, she is beaten by her flustered father. He says he's had enough fuss for one damn voting day. In this poem by Alice Walker, the heading is as important as the poem itself. It tells me that she didn't understand then, but now knows what had caused her father to do this. She understands that even though laws were passed to protect black rights, they weren't enforced at all. The lawmakers only went halfway with their actions. They made the laws, but failed to provide the means to carry them out. This was not an accident. The laws meant nothing to a white man. If he didn't want a black man to vote, then he would do something to see to it that the black man didn't vote.

Being a minority myself, I am very aware of the realities of racial prejudice, but I've never experienced them to the extent of the Blacks. I've experienced the slurs, being the butt of the joke. It made me feel ashamed of who I am. No one, I say NO ONE should EVER feel this way. Nobody should have to tell their parents to please speak English in public. Nobody should wish they were white because they get the girls—they get everything.

Blacks voting was near impossible even though laws were passed. Then the Jim Crow laws were passed to make voting hard, almost impossible for blacks. How would you feel if the law gave you a right to vote but then allowed you to be beaten or threatened if you wanted or tried to do so? This little girl was not beaten by her father; she was beaten by the man who kept him from voting.

Well now, doesn't her dad have to shoulder some of the responsibility? Do his very real problems excuse his brutality toward her? Is it okay to vent your anger on someone else? I don't think so.

Notice how you use your own experience here to help you make important meaning of this small poem. Do you think non-minority kids would see it this way? Do they have similar experiences but about different things?

What a strong statement this is!

This poem says so much to me. This tiny little poem expressed the anger, the pain, the oppression of a race. This tiny poem could serve as a whole chapter in a history book and give you a little more than just facts. Man, if Alice Walker had lived in the nineteenth century, I bet we'd have an incredibly nice world to live in. It's not the fault of the white man, but the fault of his ignorance. An Alice Walker could enlighten these people and unite the world—a world with no color lines.

or . . . she'd have been beaten down by the system. Even today she has been censored by some, her works deemed "unsuitable" for high school students to read on a state test.

Reading Response to "A Supermarket in California" by Allen Ginsberg

by Sam Otis, Grade 12: Teacher, Joan Brown

Student Response

Teacher Comments

Being gay is not a lifestyle choice; it is a state of being. People who are gay do not choose to be so; nor do they choose not to be so. It is simply who they are. Being gay is just as natural to some as being heterosexual is to others. It is not very often I read gay viewpoints in school and that is not right. The first thing I remember reading in school that was written from an openly gay point of view was a poem, "A Supermarket in California" by Allen Ginsberg. It is a poem which entails exactly what the title suggests, except what makes it stand out is the gay imagery that I, unfortunately, am not used to.

Well spoken!!

Ginsberg begins the poem with a self conscious tone. He sounds like he thinks he is being watched in a negative way, as if he is a freak. He makes reference to the full moon which is supposed to make a person crazy, and later in the poem he makes reference to Charon who is the boatman to hell. Ginsberg wrote "supermarket" in 1955, and being homosexual was viewed worse back then than it is now. He probably received harsh treatment for being himself, which led him to be so skeptical about himself. He probably wondered if he was indeed a freak, and wondered if he was going to go to hell for who he was.

What do you make of the Whitman connection, particularly given our earlier look at some Whitman poems?

It is upsetting to read something like this. The only thing Ginsberg can be accused of is being himself.

What important points you make! Such issues absolutely need to be discussed in schools, I think. Some, however, will vehemently disagree. What of them? How do schools meet the

Since he has not infringed upon the rights of anyone else, why should he feel like he is a bad person? People who are not gay and do not like gay people just because they are gay, need to stop and think for a while. These people are so incompetent, closed minded; after all, gay people do not hate heterosexual people for being attracted to people of the other sex.

Another thing I would like to mention is about using the word "straight." Who should define what "straight" is? To gay people being straight is being gay, and to heterosexuals straight is liking people of the opposite sex. If you have any decency you will never use that word for this context again.

This response is almost a brainstorm of my thoughts on this subject. There is too much to say about this, too much to think about to think about all of it now, so I tried to get a few of my stronger feelings out. I think homosexuality should be a part of the English curriculum in order for people to become acquainted with the world from a gay viewpoint. This poem was given to me from a friend of mine who is openly gay. That is probably a major reason why it has left a lasting impression on me.

needs of those who don't want to 'hear'?

A compelling and insightful response, Sam. It is a brainstorm. I can see you generating ideas as you write, and this makes your writing so very exciting to share. Thank you for your openness to risk these ideas, and for your willingness to share them.

Dialectical or Double-Entry Journal

For the simple double-entry journal, have students set up a page with two columns. In the left column, they will record or paraphrase significant words, phrases, or lines from the text they are reading. In the right column, they write their thoughts and ideas about the passages they selected.

Directions: Choose two or three passages from the poem that strike you in some way—for their meaning, the pictures they stimulate in your mind, the associations, or feelings they generate. Copy each passage in Column 1 below. In Column 2, write your response to each passage.

Example of a Double-Entry Journal in Response to the Poem "Water" by Li-Young Lee

Passage from the text	Response to the passage
In water my sister is no longer lonely. Her right leg is crooked and smaller than her left, but she swims straight. Her whole body is a glimmering fish.	*I can understand this. I think it means when we are out of our natural habitat, we can become different persons. Maybe become the people we want to be or are inside.*
Water is my father's life-sign. Son of water who'll die by water, the element which rules his life shall take it.	*I wonder if he was born in the sign of Pisces. What does this mean, he will "die by water"? I've heard of a "watery grave" but I don't think that's what he means.*

Sometimes you will want to supply the text and have students respond in the double-entry format. A useful way of teaching this kind of responding is to select a passage and create a double-entry journal response with the class, using the chalkboard or an overhead transparency. Then you might assign a specific passage for all students to respond to. A follow-up assignment would be for each student to choose two additional passages for response.

It is important for students to be clear about why they are making their selections. The generic use is to have students select passages that they think are important in some way. You can be more specific, however: Sometimes you may wish to have them select passages that are troubling, confusing; other times you might have them look for passages that reflect their own experience or feelings. When students are reading a substantial short story, a novel, or a play, they should keep a double-entry journal as they read. Some students will build a very fat journal; others will have a journal that is quite sparse. These variations point to different styles of processing information during reading and are not to be interpreted as "the more entries, the better." It is more important to look at the quality of selection and response, guiding students individually as you see them missing opportunities or including too much tangential material.

There are, of course, many variations on this basic double-entry journal. Here is one format incorporating a graphic element that is especially useful when working with a difficult text:

Passage from Text	What I think it means	Quick Sketch	Explanation of Sketch

Using this format, students begin by explaining the text; then they make a sketch of something that helps them crystallize the meaning. The drawing might be a realistic reproduction of a key image in the text or it might be something that symbolizes the meaning of the passage. In the last column, the student writes a brief explanation of the sketch , telling how it focuses the meaning of the passage.

Applying the Rubric: The Teacher as Mindful Observer

The teacher's role in teaching not just literature but the *reading* of literature has not yet reached the level of sophistication of that of the teacher's role in teaching not just writing but the processes involved in writing. To reach the level of master teachers, we must become *mindful observers* at several levels: We must first become mindful observers of ourselves as we plan how we will assign and teach works of literature; then we must become mindful observers of our students as they engage in the processes of creating their own understanding of a work. In addition to becoming aware of the many dimensions of creating literature for ourselves and our students, we must also help students learn to become mindful observers of their own ways of reading, not only the texts of our classrooms but also the texts of the world. In later chapters you will find some suggestions of how to handle the logistics of both student self-assessment and teacher evaluation.

Applying the Rubric: The Teacher as Archeologist

Regardless of how we may see ourselves as careful observers of our students as readers, the fact remains that a large part of assessment is based on student products. By far the most prevalent product for the assessment of reading is what a student writes in response to that reading. In the previous sections, we dealt largely with informal written responses and informal (although carefully recorded) teacher observations, based largely on established reading performances. However comfortable teachers are with informal assessments, it is important to be able to articulate our evaluations in a more formal means of assessment. Our long tradition of formal evaluation of student writing has not prepared us to evaluate reading when it is defined as the process of constructing meaning. To use a scaled rubric such as the one in this chapter, teachers must become archeologists, learning to look carefully at each student notation and drawing as well as the more sustained written responses. This rubric is applied holistically; that is, the entire student response is taken into consideration before a score is assigned. In some cases, a paper rich in margin notes may receive a high score, even though much of the test paper is blank. If the evidence of an insightful, discerning reading is present, wherever it is found, the paper receives a high score.

To see how teachers can apply the rubric to the actual artifacts and bones of student response, the written and drawn evidence of reading, here are three student papers, representing score points 6, 4, and 2 using the rubric presented in this chapter. Each paper was scored by two or more highly trained teachers using the 6-point scale. Following each student paper is a brief commentary explaining how the paper reflects its score point. These papers were written by tenth-grade students during one class period under highly controlled testing conditions. The commentary, used by teachers in scoring sessions and staff development, was written by Laura Wade, a teacher serving as Chief Reader in the statewide scoring session where this prompt was used.

The first paper was written by Nhu Chau, a sophomore at Andrew P. Hill High School in a large urban district of San Jose, California. Teachers in this district have clearly incorporated many diverse reading strategies in their teaching of literature. Here is Nhu's paper, followed by an evaluator's commentary.

Section One
Reading

Before You Read

You are going to read an excerpt from a story by contemporary California writer Gerald Haslam.

Reading Selection

Excerpt from The Horned Toad
by Gerald Haslam

My thoughts and/or
questions about
what I am reading

"*Expectoran su sangre!*" exclaimed Great-grandma when I showed her the small horned toad I had removed from my breast pocket. I turned toward my mother, who translated: "They spit blood."

I am confused with the Spanish.

"*De los ojos,*" Grandma added. "From their eyes," mother explained, herself uncomfortable in the presence of the small beast.

What does the lizard have to do with the story?

I grinned, "Awwwwww."

But my Great-grandmother did not smile. "*Son muy toxicos,*" she nodded with finality. Mother moved back an involuntary step, her hands suddenly busy at her breast. "Put that thing down," she ordered.

In the discussion, there is a visable barrier between the four generations. One has the knowledge. the other has the concern. And the youngest has the ignorance of youth.

"His name's John," I said.

"Put John down and not in your pocket, either," my mother nearly shouted. "Those things are very poisonous. Didn't you understand what Grandma said?"

I shook my head.

"Well..." mother looked from one of us to the other—spanning four generations of California, standing three feet apart—and said, "of course you didn't. Please take him back where you got him, and be careful. We'll all feel better when you do." The tone of her voice told me that the discussion had ended, so I released the little reptile where I'd captured him.

During those years in Oildale, the mid-1940s, I needed only to walk across the street to find a patch of virgin desert. Neighborhood kids called it simply "the vacant lot," less than an acre without houses or sidewalks. Not that we were desperate for desert then, since we could walk into its scorched skin a mere half-mile west, north, and east. To the south, incongruously, flowed the icy Kern River, fresh from the Sierras and surrounded by riparian forest.

That spring, when I discovered the lone horned toad near the back of the lot, had been rough on my family. Earlier, there had been quiet, unpleasant tension between Mom and Daddy. He was a silent man, little given to emotional displays. It was difficult for him to show affection and I guess the openness of Mom's family made him uneasy. Daddy had no kin in California and rarely mentioned any in Texas. He couldn't seem to understand my mother's large, intimate family, their constant noisy concern for one another, and I think he was a little jealous of the time she gave everyone, maybe even me.

I heard her talking on the phone to my various aunts and uncles, usually in Spanish. Even though I couldn't understand—Daddy had warned her not to teach me that foreign tongue because it would hurt me in school, and she'd complied—I could sense the stress. I had been afraid they were going to divorce, since she only used Spanish to hide things from me. I'd confronted her with my suspicion, but she comforted me, saying, no, that was not the problem. They were merely deciding when it would be our turn to care for Grandma. I didn't really understand, although I was relieved.

I later learned that my Great-grandmother—whom we simply called "Grandma"—had been moving from house to house within the family, trying to find a place she'd accept. She hated the city, and most of the aunts and uncles lived in Los Angeles. She had wanted to come to our place right away because she had raised my mother from a baby when my own grandmother died. But the old lady seemed unimpressed with Daddy, whom she called "ese gringo."

In truth, we had more room, and my dad made more money in the oil patch than almost anyone else in the family. Since my mother was the closest to Grandma, our place was the logical one for her, but Ese Gringo didn't see it that way, I guess, at least not at first. Finally, after much debate, he relented.

In any case, one windy afternoon, my Uncle Manuel and Aunt Toni drove up and deposited four-and-a-half feet of bewigged, bejeweled Spanish spitfire; a square, pale

My thoughts and/or questions about what I am reading

I can understand his dad feeling unaccustomed to the family and left out of his mothers life. although his act does show some immaturity.

I wonder why he doesn't want his son to learn Spanish. or should don't hurt him in school.

It's sad to see older people being shipped from place to place.

face topped by a tightly-curled black wig that hid a bald head—her hair having been lost to typhoid nearly sixty years before—her small white hands veined with rivers of blue. She walked with a prancing bounce that made her appear half her age, and she barked orders in Spanish from the moment she emerged from Manuel and Toni's car. Later, just before they left, I heard Uncle Manuel tell my dad, "Good luck, Charlie. That old lady's dynamite." Daddy only grunted.

She had been with us only two days when I tried to impress her with my horned toad. In fact, nothing I did seemed to impress her, and she referred to me as *el malcriado*, causing my mother to shake her head. Mom explained to me that Grandma was just old and lonely for Grandpa and uncomfortable in town.

As it turned out, I didn't really understand very much about Grandma at all. She was old, of course, yet in many ways my parents treated her as though she were younger than me, walking her to the bathroom at night and bringing her presents from the store. In other ways—drinking wine at dinner, for example · she was granted adult privileges. Even Daddy didn't drink wine except on special occasions. After Grandma moved in, though, he began to occasionally join her for a glass, sometimes even sitting with her on the porch for a premeal sip.

This action is not untypical with many. Age is not ignorance.

One afternoon I returned from school and saw Grandma perched on the porch as usual, so I started to walk around the house to avoid her sharp, mostly incomprehensible, tongue. She had already spotted me. "*Venga aquí!*" she ordered, and I understood.

I approached the porch and noticed that Grandma was vigorously chewing something. She held a small white bag in one hand. Saying "*Qué deseas tomar?*" she withdrew a large orange gumdrop from the bag and began slowly chewing it in her toothless mouth, smacking loudly as she did so. I stood below her for a moment trying to remember the word for candy. Then it came to me: "*Dulce,*" I said.

I like the way the Grandma is trying to teach him Spanish.

Still chewing, Grandma replied "*Mande?*"

Knowing she wanted a complete sentence, I again struggled, then came up with "*Deseo dulce.*"

She measured me for a moment, before answering in nearly perfect English, "Oh, so you wan' some candy. Go to the store an' buy some."

I don't know if it was the shock of hearing her speak English for the first time, or the way she had denied me a piece of candy, but I suddenly felt tears warm my cheeks and I sprinted into the house and found Mom, who stood at the kitchen sink. "Grandma just talked English," I burst between light sobs.

"What's wrong?" she asked as she reached out to stroke my head.

"Grandma can talk English," I repeated.

"Of course she can," Mom answered. "What's wrong?"

I wasn't sure what was wrong, but after considering, I told Mom that Grandma had teased me. No sooner had I said that than the old woman appeared at the door.

"Do not weep, little one," the old lady comforted me, "Jesus and the Virgin love you." She smiled and patted my head. To my mother she said as though just realizing it, "Your baby?"

Somehow that day changed everything. I wasn't afraid of my great-grandmother any longer and, once I began spending time with her on the porch, I realized that my father had also begun directing increased attention to the old woman. Almost every evening Ese Gringo was sharing wine with Grandma. They talked out there, but I never did hear a real two-way conversation between them. Usually Grandma rattled on and Daddy nodded. She'd chuckle and pat his hand and he might grin, even grunt a word or two, before she'd begin talking again. Once I saw my mother standing by the front window watching them together, a smile playing across her face.

No more did I sneak around the house to avoid Grandma after school. Instead, she waited for me and discussed my efforts in class gravely, telling mother that I was a bright boy, "muy inteligente," and that I should be sent to the nuns who would train me. I would make a fine priest. When Ese Gringo heard that, he smiled and said, "He'd make a fair-to-middlin' Holy Roller preacher, too." Even Mom had to chuckle, and my great-grandmother shook her finger at Ese Gringo. "Oh you debil, Sharlie!" she cackled.

Because she liked the lot and the things that grew there, I showed her the horned toad when I captured it a second time. I was determined to keep it, although I did not discuss my plans with anyone. I also wanted to hear more about the bloody eyes, so I thrust the small animal nearly into her face one afternoon. She did not flinch. "Ola señor sangre de ojos," she said with a mischievous grin. "Qué tal?" It took me a moment to catch on.

My thoughts and/or questions about what I am reading

After the barrier of communication broke, Haslam began to understand his grandmother. Out of that understanding grew a friendship.

They are beginning to accept the new addition to the family.

Haslam no longer avoids this grandmother after beginning to understand her.

"You were kidding before," I accused.

"Of course," she acknowledged, still grinning.

"But why?"

"Because the little beast belongs with his own kind in his own place, not in your pocket. Give him his freedom, my son."

I had other plans for the horned toad, but I was clever enough not to cross Grandma. "Yes, Ma'am," I replied. That night I placed the reptile in a flower bed cornered by a brick wall Ese Gringo had built the previous summer. It was a spot rich with insects for the toad to eat, and the little wall, only a foot high, must have seemed massive to so squat an animal.

Nonetheless, the next morning when I searched for the horned toad it was gone. I had no time to explore the yard for it, so I trudged off to school, my belly troubled. How could it have escaped? Classes meant little to me that day. I thought only of my lost pet—I had changed his name to Juan, the same as my Great-grandfather—and where I might find him.

I shortened my conversation with Grandma that afternoon so I could search for Juan. "What do you seek?" the old woman asked me as I poked through flower beds beneath the porch. "Praying mantises," I improvised, and she merely nodded, surveying me. But I had eyes only for my lost pet, and I continued pushing through branches and brushing aside leaves. No luck.

Finally, I gave in and turned toward the lot. I found my horned toad nearly across the street, crushed. It had been heading for the miniature desert and had almost made it when an automobile's tire had run over it. One notion immediately swept me: if I had left it on its lot, it would still be alive. I stood rooted there in the street, tears slicking my cheeks, and a car honked its horn as it passed, the driver shouting at me.

Grandma joined me, and stroked my back. "The poor little beast," was all she said, then she bent slowly and scooped up what remained of the horned toad and led me out of the street. "We must return him to his own place," she explained, and we trooped, my eyes still clouded, toward the back of the vacant lot. Carefully, I dug a hole with a piece of wood. Grandma placed Juan in it and covered him. We said an Our Father and a Hail Mary, then Grandma walked me back to the house. "Your little Juan is safe with God, my son," she comforted. We kept the

My thoughts and/or questions about what I am reading

The Grandma may be a parallel to the toad when she said that the toad belongs to his own kind, I have the feeling that she may be talking about herself

This may be foreshadowing the grandmother's death. The guilt that Harlam felt may be parallel to the guilt that the family will feel.

Again, the grandmother seems to have an extensive knowledge of things out of their place.

horned toad's death a secret, and we visited his small grave frequently.

Grandma fell just before school ended and summer vacation began. As was her habit, she had walked alone to the vacant lot but this time, on her way back, she tripped over the curb and broke her hip. That following week, when Daddy brought her home from the hospital, she seemed to have shrunken. She sat hunched in a wheelchair on the porch, gazing with faded eyes toward the hills or at the lot, speaking rarely. She still sipped wine every evening with Daddy and even I could tell how concerned he was about her. It got to where he'd look in on her before leaving for work every morning and again at night before turning in. And if Daddy was home, Grandma always wanted him to push her chair when she needed moving, calling, "Sharlie!" until he arrived.

I was tugged from sleep on the night she died by voices drumming through the walls into darkness. I couldn't understand them, but was immediately frightened by the uncommon sounds of words in the night. I struggled from bed and walked into the living room just as Daddy closed the front door and a car pulled away.

Mom was sobbing softly on the couch and Daddy walked to her, stroked her head, then noticed me. "Come here, son," he gently ordered.

I walked to him and, uncharacteristically, he put an arm around me. "What's wrong?" I asked, near tears myself. Mom looked up, but before she could speak, Daddy said, "Grandma died." Then he sighed heavily and stood there with his arms around his weeping wife and son.

The next day my Uncle Manuel and Uncle Arnulfo, plus Aunt Chintia, arrived and over food they discussed with my mother where Grandma should be interred. They argued that it would be too expensive to transport her body home and, besides, they could more easily visit her grave if she was buried in Bakersfield. "They have such a nice, manicured grounds at Greenlawn," Aunt Chintia pointed out. Just when it seemed they had agreed, I could remain silent no longer. "But Grandma has to go home," I burst. "She has to! It's the only thing she really wanted. We can't leave her in the city."

Uncle Arnulfo, who was on the edge, snapped to Mother that I belonged with the other children, not interrupting adult conversation. Mom quietly agreed, but

My thoughts and/or
questions about
what I am reading

It is similar the way the Grandma falls and the toad dies, all are connected to the industrialized transportation system.

The fact that she is looking towards the hills or lot seems to suggest that she is longing to be there or that she belongs there.

Like the toad, the boy understands that his Grandma must be buried where she belongs.

I refused. My father walked into the room then. "What's wrong?" he asked.

"They're going to bury Grandma in Bakersfield, Daddy. Don't let em, please."

"Well, son..."

"When my horny toad got killed and she helped me to bury it, she said we had to return him to his place."

"Your horny toad?" Mother asked.

"He got squished and me and Grandma buried him in the lot. She said we had to take him back to his place. Honest she did."

No one spoke for a moment, then my father, Ese Gringo, who stood against the sink, responded: "That's right..." he paused, then added, "We'll bury her." I saw a weary smile cross my mother's face. "If she wanted to go back to the ranch then that's where we have to take her," Daddy said.

I hugged him and he, right in front of everyone, hugged back.

No one argued. It seemed, suddenly, as though they had all wanted to do exactly what I had begged for. Grown-ups baffled me. Late that week the entire family, hundreds it seemed, gathered at the little Catholic church in Coalinga for mass, then drove out to Arroyo Cantua and buried Grandma next to Grandpa. She rests there today.

My mother, father, and I drove back to Oildale that afternoon across the scorching westside desert, through sand and tumbleweeds and heat shivers. Quiet and sad, we knew we had done our best. Mom, who usually sat next to the door in the front seat, snuggled close to Daddy, and I heard her whisper to him, "Thank you, Charlie," as she kissed his cheek.

Daddy squeezed her, hesitated as if to clear his throat, then answered, "When you're family, you take care of your own."

My thoughts and/or questions about what I am reading

again, the horned toad incident is a parallel to what happens to Grandma. It is also something that Haslam learns from and uses later on in his life.

Haslam, Gerald. "The Horned Toad" from *California Childhood: Recollections & Stories of the Golden State.* Berkeley, Creative Arts Book Company, 1988, pp. 139-145.

After You Have Read

Now that you have finished reading the selection, respond as fully as you can to the following questions and activities. You may refer to the reading selection as often as you like.

1. What is your first response to the story? Take a few minutes to write your ideas, questions, or opinions.

Hoolam story is very touching. It makes me to see that the adults were talking of Grandma's burial place as if it were an evening out at the movies. They were arranging it just for convenience sake.

I am amazed by the way the horn toad incident fits into the death of Grandma. It is through this incident that the adults themselves realize that they should abide by what Grandma would have wanted. Tholam brilliantly connected these two events, using one to foreshadow the other and to create a parallel to the other situation.

Tholam's writing is very simple, yet it expresses a lesson that we may one day have to learn. He teaches us that people must be in a place where they belong.

2. Below is a double-entry journal. In Column One, copy one or two brief passages from the
   story that you think are important to the story. In Column Two, explain why you think
   they are important.

Column One	Column Two
Passages from the story	My thoughts
"Because the little beast belongs with his own kind. Give him his freedom, my son."	This forshadows Grandmas death and suggest that the Gandma feels that she should be with her own kind. It suggest that she wanted to be where she belong. It also establishes her view of this subject.
"But Grandma has to go home She has to! It is the only thing she really wanted. We cant leave her in the city."	This shows the impact the Grandmas teachings had on the boy. It shows how her belief and vigor of this subject is passed on to him.

3. In the outlines below, use symbols, images, drawings, and/or words to show what either the boy or his father was thinking or feeling at the <u>beginning</u> of the story and at the <u>end</u> of the story.

The character I choose is: ☑ the boy   ☐ his father

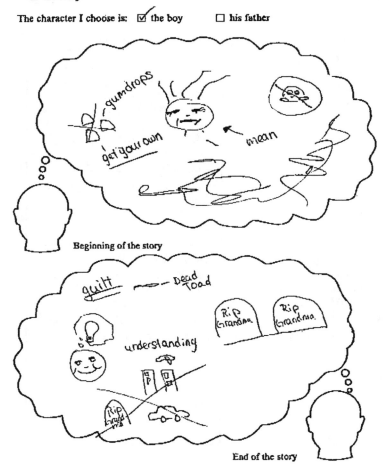

Beginning of the story

End of the story

4. Explain how your symbols, images, drawings, and/or words represent your ideas about what the boy or his father are thinking and feeling.

In the beginning the boy felt that his grandma is crabby. My picture portrays this. He knew that the toad was off limits and my picture of the frog with the cross reveals this. Overall, he couldn't really understand his grandma. The dark clouds symbolize confusion.

In the end when the toad dies he feels guilt. He also learns a lesson from his Grandma. The light bulb symbolizes his understanding of that lesson. The last two pictures show that he is determined to have Grandma buried by Grandpa and not in the city.

5. Look back at your responses to questions 3 and 4. Now write about how the character does or does not change.

The character changes because of the toad incident. Through this, his grandma teaches that one must be where one belongs. Through this, the character has matured mentally and is able to understand and element that even the adults have neglected; that Grandma should be buried at home where she belongs.

6. Most stories involve several conflicts or difficulties and a resolution of a central conflict. What conflict in "The Horned Toad" do you find most interesting or important? It may be the central conflict of the story or some minor conflict. Tell about the conflict you chose, explain why you find it so interesting or important, and tell how this conflict was or was not resolved.

Conflict in story and its importance:

The most interesting conflict for me was the main one; the decision of where Grandma is to be buried. It is important because it shows how Grandma's life has made an impact on the boy's life. Without her he would have been ignorant of the lesson that she teaches him.

How the conflict was/was not resolved:

The conflict is resolved when the boy explains to his family about the toad incident. He insist that Grandma, like the toad, deserves to be buried where she belongs. He states that being at home was all she ever wanted. The adults soon realizes their foolishness and decides to bury her at home.

7. This is your chance to write anything else you want about this story—what it means to you, what it reminds you of, or whatever else you think is important.

Like the funeral arrangements in this story, I feel that in todays society, people are beginning to arrange the funerals according to their wants and desires instead of the deceased. This trend is selfish and inconsiderate. The least one can do is to consider what the person would have wanted in the funeral.

This story also brings up how one incident may be of some help later on in life. At first, the toad incident may seem like an unimportant event but it taught the boy a lesson that he will never forget. It helped him to be wise enough to speak for his grandmother about her funeral arrangement.

This story also expresses how one person can change one's life. The boy changed drastically after his grandmother came. The lesson at the end proves what a great impact she has on him

STOP!

This is the end of Section One.

Reading Assessment
Illustrative Essay Commentary

Prompt Title _____ **Horned Toad** _____

Paper Numbe _____

Score Point _____ 6

Commentary Writer _____ **Laura Wade** _____

The evidence provided in this response indicates an exemplary reading performance. Immediately in the first margin note, the reader is perceptive as to the complexities of the text: "There is a visable barrier between the four generations. One has the knowledge. The other has the concern. And the youngest has the ignorance of youth." In a later margin note, the reader comments, "It's sad to see older people being shipped from place to place." The reader has drawn on evidence from the text to reflect on his own ideas. As additional information becomes available, the reader explores multiple possibilities of meaning, grounding these meanings in his acute perceptions. "After the barrier of communication broke, Haslam began to understand his grandmother. Out of that understanding grew a friendship." As this reader constructs meaning in the text, he understands the whole work as well as an awareness of how the parts work together to create the whole. "The Grandma may be a parrallel to the toad when she said that the toad belongs to his own kind. I have the feeling that she may be talking about herself....This may be foreshadowing the grandmother's death. The guilt that Haslam felt may be parallel to the guilt that the family will feel." The reader is insightful as to the actions of the grandmother. "The fact that she is looking towards the hills or lot seems to suggest that she is longing to be there or that she belongs there." This reader validates the author's style saying, "Haslam's writing is very simple, yet it expresses a lesson that we may one day have to learn. He teaches us that people must be in a place where they belong." The graphics in the open minds along with their explanations demonstrate a perceptive understanding of the boy and his feelings. The use of the dark clouds and the light bulb as symbols show how the reader draws on evidence from the text and expands and reflects on his own ideas. The reader also articulates a newly developed level of understanding in his final response when discussing the idea of arranging funerals and how one person can change one's life.

Overall, this paper demonstrates an exemplary reading performance that is insightful, discerning and perceptive.

This student responded to only two questions in the reading prompt. The remaining pages of the student booklet have not been reproduced.

After You Have Read

Now that you have finished reading the selection, respond as fully as you can to the following questions and activities. You may refer to the reading selection as often as you like.

1. What is your first response to the story? Take a few minutes to write your ideas, questions, or opinions.

I feel that it was a benefit for the grandmother to come to their home. In the beginning, the father and mother seemed at odds with each other and the poor boy didn't feel like he had a happy family. It was anticapated that the grandmother moving in would make matters worse but it didn't. the family was closer and happy again, even when she died, they stayed a happy family. the Grandmother was a great part in the boys life. I think when she helped him bury the toad in "his place", it taught the boy exactly what his father said in the end, "when you're family you take care of your own". It's a lesson the boy will probably never forget.

2. Below is a double-entry journal. In Column One, copy one or two brief passages from the story that you think are important to the story. In Column Two, explain why you think they are important.

Column One	Column Two
Passages from the story	My thoughts
"I hugged him and he, right in front of everyone, hugged back"	this shows how, with every bad thing, something comes out with the grandmother's death, the father and son were closer than they'd ever been.
"when you're family, you take care of your own"	family is the most important thing. when you have your family with you, you take care of eachother, and love eachother. Be there for them, as they would for you.

3. In the outlines below, use symbols, images, drawings, and/or words to show what either the boy or his father was thinking or feeling at the beginning of the story and at the end of the story.

The character I choose is: ☑ the boy   ☐ his father

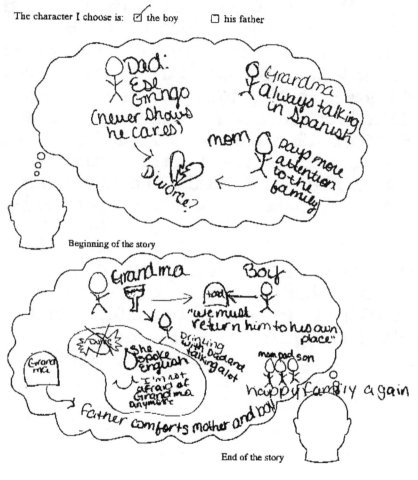

Beginning of the story

End of the story

4. Explain how your symbols, images, drawings, and/or words represent your ideas about what the boy or his father are thinking and feeling.

The father and mother aren't communicated bicause the father feels like mother his more attention to the family which makes the boy feel like his parents might divorce. He dousn't think grandma's stay is a good idea. But when she comes she gets along with dad. When she speaks english about the candy, he's not afraid of her anyone. When she buried the toad it brings them closer when she dies, it brings him, mom and dad, Closer as a family

5. Look back at your responses to questions 3 and 4. Now write about how the character does or does not change.

His ideas about his father and grandmother changes. He and the grandmother become friends. He sees the caring side of his dad.

6. Most stories involve several conflicts or difficulties and a resolution of a central conflict. What conflict in "The Horned Toad" do you find most interesting or important? It may be the central conflict of the story or some minor conflict. Tell about the conflict you chose, explain why you find it so interesting or important, and tell how this conflict was or was not resolved.

Conflict in story and its importance:

I think when the "Horned toad" died and the Grandma buried him was the most important conflict I think the conflict was when the adults wanted to bury the grandma in the city but the boy said she should be buried in her place. It was resolved when his father agreed they hugged and everyone else agreed as well. It's important to listen to youre family and don't count anyone out.

How the conflict was/was not resolved:

the family buried the grandma in her place next to the grandfather

7. This is your chance to write anything else you want about this story—what it means to you, what it reminds you of, or whatever else you think is important.

It just proves how strong and important family is to me. Family is one of the greatest gifts and you should always try to savor it.

STOP!

This is the end of Section One.

Reading Assessment
Illustrative Essay Commentary

Prompt Title _____ **Horned Toad** _____

Paper Number _____

Score Point _____ **4** _____

Commentary Writer _____ **Laura Wade** _____

The evidence provided in this response indicates a thoughtful reading performance. The reader fills in the gaps in the text, making assumptions from cues in the text. This is clearly seen in the first response: "'The Grandmother was a great part in the boy's life. I think when she helped him bury the toad in 'his place,' it taught the boy exactly what his father said in the end, 'When you're family you take care of your own.' It's a lesson the boy will probably never forget." The reader also demonstrates a thoughtful response to the passage "I hugged him and he, right in front of everyone, hugged back" by responding, "This shows how, with every bad thing, something comes out with the grandmother's death, the father and son were closer than they'd ever been." The reader expands on ideas in the text, but with less depth than higher score points. This is seen again in the second response to a text passage. The reader states, "Family is the most important thing. When you have your family with you, you take care of each other, and love each other. Be there for them as they would for you." The reader also tends to retell and paraphrase, often thoroughly and purposefully, but he accepts the text without exploring multiple possibilities of meaning. He tends to present his understanding of the text as fixed and does not revise his interpretation as additional information becomes available. This reader thoughtfully focuses on the family and how "It just proves how strong and important family is to me. Family is one of the greatest gifts and you should always try to savor it." This personal connection demonstrates a more general significance than just the literal facts of the text. Overall, this reader constructs a thoughtful and plausible interpretation of the text.

The Question of a Valid Interpretation

One question that will be and needs to be raised in any discussion of assessing a student's interpretation of a work of literature is the question of validity. If you subscribe to the theory that interpretation is a

After You Have Read

Now that you have finished reading the selection, respond as fully as you can to the following questions and activities. You may refer to the reading selection as often as you like.

1. What is your first response to the story? Take a few minutes to write your ideas, questions, or opinions.

The story that I just finished read here was talking about the Grandma, John and the Horned Toad. What I Know about this story is that John father never like his wife Grandmother and the way they talk to each other in spanish. But there were some words that were hard to read like the spanish words.

2. Below is a double-entry journal. In Column One, copy one or two brief passages from the story that you think are important to the story. In Column Two, explain why you think they are important.

Column One	Column Two
Passages from the story	My thoughts
If I had left it on it lot, it would	

Reading Assessment
Illustrative Essay Commentary

Prompt Title _____ **Horned Toad** _____

Paper Number _____

Score Point ____ **2** _____

Commentary Writer ____ **Laura Wade** _____

The evidence provided in this response indicates a limited reading performance. The reader constructs partial meaning for the text: "The story that I just finished read here was talking about the Grandma, John and the Horned Toad. What I know about this story is that John father never like his wife Grandmother and they way they talk to each other in Spanish." This reader reduces the meanings of the text to demonstrate only a superficial understanding of part of the text. By overgeneralizing and oversimplifying, the reader seems unable to grasp the whole. This reader's performance could improve with responses to the multiple activities following the text, thus demonstrating the ability to construct meaning from interacting with text.

Overall, this paper is a clear example of a limited reading performance.

matter of discovering the author's intent and elaborating on it, then the question is, how does anyone know the author's intent? If you subscribe to the belief that all meaning resides in the words on the page, then it is simply a matter of agreeing on the definitions of those words. But when you subscribe to a definition of reading as the construction of meaning, the question of validity becomes very real indeed. There is a plethora of critics who declare this approach to be the Humpty Dumpty version of interpretation: A poem means whatever I want it to mean. This criticism is unfounded, however, and needs to be met with very clear criteria as to what constitutes, in the words of the scoring guide in this chapter, a "warranted and responsible" interpretation.

These quotations from Louise Rosenblatt's article "The Transactional Theory: Against Dualisms" in *College English*, April '93, have been particularly helpful to me in discussing the question of "valid" interpretations of texts. I certainly could not express it more succinctly:

> John Dewey . . . contributes the idea of "warranted assertibility" in scientific inquiry. What conditions or operations warrant or justify an assertion as "true"? Agreed-upon criteria for what constitute sound methods of inquiry and judgment make possible agreement on "warranted," though tentative answers. . . . If we agree on criteria for validity of interpretation, we can decide on the most defensible interpretation or interpretations. . . . This leaves open the possibility of equally valid alternative interpretations as well as alternative criteria for validity of interpretations. Such an approach enables us to present a sophisticated understanding of the openness and constraints of language to our students without abnegating the possibility of responsible reading of texts.

The assessment of reading, while isolated in this chapter for purposes of focus, should rarely be thought of as separate from the other aspects of the English curriculum. Reading is so closely aligned with thinking (not that one must read to think, but that one must think to read) that any evaluation of reading is, by its very nature, also an evaluation of a student's ability to articulate orally, to engage in interpersonal problem solving, and/or, to some degree at least, to write. With the caveat, then, that it is the whole person who uses reading, writing, speech, and listening behavior to demonstrate literacy, we turn, in the next chapter, to look specifically at the assigning and assessing of writing. In later chapters, we will look at how both reading and writing fit into an integrated approach to teaching and assessing student literacy.

Chapter Three

Assigning and Assessing Writing

Rough Draft

I wring this poem
Like a wet rag, to bare
Essential, but I can't ever
Quite squeeze the rag
Completely dry. Rough
Drafts never smooth
Perfectly, after all, just
Even out to infinitesimal
Graininess, n-sided polygons
Disguised as circles.
Or (perhaps) they really
Metamorphose, as caterpillars
Will. If so, the final
Crisp wing conceals
Startling transfigurations.

Initial gropings, then:
The blind, deaf hand
Feeling the touch of water,
merely, and nothing less than,
The journey to poetry.
—Freeman Ng

Freeman Ng, who has long since grown up, wrote "Rough Draft" when he was a junior in high school. At that time he was a brilliant, budding physicist, assured of a favored place at the university of his choice. He was also a brilliant, already-flowering poet, but he fought against that propensity, harshly critical of his work, resisting the effect of his poems on those of us who saw what was happening. "Initial gropings," he calls them here, as he struggles against the "journey to poetry." But he couldn't withstand the power that working with these rough drafts had on his mind and, midway through his freshman year at the University of California, Berkeley, Freeman returned to my classroom one day to admit that he had given in. He had changed his major to English. I would have been no less pleased to have a poet masquerading as a theoretical physicist working on the mysteries of the universe; I have long seen the alliance between the two fields. But for Freeman, the change was a profound one and bears testimony to the power of the act of writing.

It is this power that we tap whenever we ask our students to write. It is this power that we exercise every time we write comments on a student's paper. It is the effects of this power that we must somehow be able to help our students perceive to be within their reach. They must have access to it, be able to use it for whatever their own individual needs may be. Not many of them will become theoretical physicists. Fewer will become poets. But they can all know the results that Helen Keller experienced when "the blind, deaf hand" felt "the touch of water" and learned not only that there is such a thing as language, but that she had the power of using it, making it suit her purposes.

During the last twenty or so years, we have become increasingly more sophisticated in our understanding of this power that seems to lie within language. We have studied the way people write, observing ourselves and our students participate in the processes of thinking, drafting, re-thinking, re-drafting, re-visioning, and, if we carry a project through, editing for some kind of publication. "This is my letter to the world," Emily Dickinson wrote, even as she bound up her poems and made her sister promise to destroy them at her death. An ambiguous message. What can we make of it that might impact the way we use writing in the classroom? What does it say to us about the power that we wield when we assign and assess the writing of our students?

Writing and Purpose

One of the ways that we can use our increased knowledge about what we do when we write is to be sure that all of our assignments are built upon the concept of *purpose*. We know that purpose drives writing, as it drives so much else in our lives. We know that human beings have the potential for creating a great many purposes for writing, each of which leads to a piece with identifiable features. It is these features that distinguish what some call *discourse types* or *writing domains* but which we will refer to throughout this book simply as *writing types*. By involving students in learning to articulate their purposes for writing, and then to understand how different purposes require different approaches, we can teach them how to become thinking or *transactive* writers. With a clear sense of audience and purpose, and with an understanding of the features that characterize writing for different purposes, students can engage in productive writing response groups and learn the art of true revision rather than recopying with superficial corrections. The resulting pieces, then, can be evaluated both by teachers and students as they work from the same premises of what constitutes an effective piece of a particular kind or type of writing.

The concept of *writing type* is subtly different from that of *genre*. A writing type, as I am using it in this book, is distinguished by author purpose rather than by the stylistic or formal features of a genre. The model in Figure 3-1 depicting four global writing types combines Jimmy Britton's ideas with Louise Rosenblatt's aesthetic/efferent continuum. In Britton's model, expressive writing is the groundwork that gives rise to both transactional (writing for purposes of communicating specific information) and poetic writing (writing for aesthetic purposes). Rosenblatt's model, also built on the idea of writer purpose, shows aesthetic and efferent purposes at the extremes but indicates that purpose is a matter of emphasis rather than exclusion. This model evolved as a group of classroom teachers worked together to develop a statewide writing assessment program in California; in the years since its widespread use in staff development workshops, it has proven useful for classroom teachers. By helping students identify the naturally occurring features of these four global writing types, we are also teaching students to be able to identify the features that will form the bases for their own, their peers', and their teachers' evaluations of their work.

This model is designed to encompass the variety of purposes for which both children and adults write. It acknowledges that expressive writing is foundational to all the other types. The additional categories describe purposes that evolve from and build on *expressive* writing: *persuasive, informative or efferent,* and *literary or aesthetic* writing. There is considerable overlap among the types; persuasive writing, for instance, often moves into the aesthetic realm when it is carefully crafted. In setting up assignments to teach

Figure 3-1

Global Writing Types

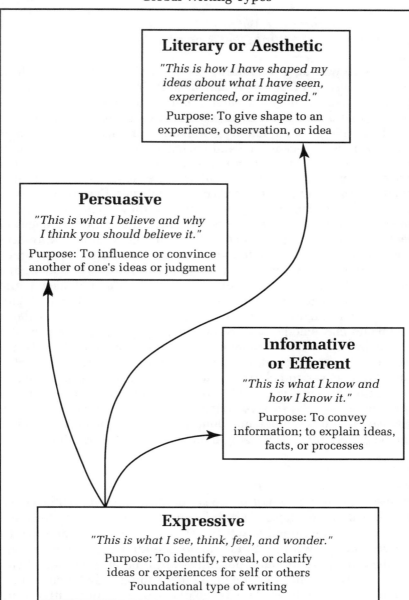

particular writing features, however, the types provide a sound theoretical framework.

Expressive Writing: "This is what I see, think, feel, and wonder."

Expressive writing is a natural kind of writing dealing with ideas, observations, and feelings. It may describe a scene or focus on the personal significance of a person, object, or memory. It includes writing that is done for the self, like diary or journal entries, as well as pieces like personal letters or reflective passages intended to be read by friends. Because the audience may be the self or an outside reader, purposes for creating expressive pieces vary widely. These purposes may be descriptive, reflective, or exploratory in nature; such pieces often incorporate narrative strategies. Expressive writers may begin to consider aesthetic features as they reach out to friends to convey a vivid impression of thoughts, remembered images or feelings, and the significance of their thoughts. Since expressive writing provides a foundation for aesthetic, persuasive, and informative writing, it may embody such narrative strategies as action, dialogue, and chronological sequencing, as well as persuasive and informative language. When shaped and composed for an audience beyond that of close friends, such writing moves into the aesthetic realm and may emerge as story, autobiography, poem, or essay.

Its importance developmentally cannot be overemphasized because it allows emergent writers to use writing as a way to develop fluency, discover and clarify what they think, and engage in reflective explorations. Teachers facilitate writing development when they encourage expressive writing through journals, reading response logs, and writer's notebooks, and when they give students the responsibility for choosing their own topics for writing.

Assessing expressive writing

Assessing expressive writing does not quite constitute an oxymoron, but it comes close. Certainly journals and reading logs and other kinds of expressive writing should never be graded for the conventions of writing. Since this is the kind of writing that engenders the more formal types, however, it is important to let students know not only that we value their doing it, but also that we value specific qualities. This is the place to respond positively, informally, by writing notes to the student either in the margins or on Post-its™, if we do not wish to intrude permanently on the student's writing. What do we look for in these free-ranging journals or logs? Here are some starters:

Fluency: Expressive writing encourages fluency. In classes where teachers have given students five or ten minutes daily simply to write freely in their journals, teachers have seen fluency increase dramatically in just a few weeks. For second-language learners especially, achieving fluency is the first step toward control. We want to encourage and give positive responses to increased fluency.

Use of Concrete Language and Sensory Detail: Every type of writing depends for its effectiveness on specificity. "Not ideas about the thing, but the thing itself," Wallace Stevens wrote. Look for examples of close observation, recorded dialogue, sensory language. Point out examples that show precise use of language.

Reflectiveness: Expressive writing naturally leads to reflections. Encourage students to explore their ideas, noting when they may lead to new insights. Look for risk-taking as students move into unfamiliar territory reflecting on things they have seen, done, thought, and felt.

All of these suggestions involve responding to student writing. The realities, of course, include the fact that, especially at the middle and high school levels, it is impossible to respond to all of the expressive writing that we expect students to do. There are a number of ways to deal with this student writing overload: For reading logs and journals, it is useful to have students themselves mark which selections they want you to read. You may set up a pattern whereby you read at least three entries a week, reading more if your time allows. In some situations, it is useful to give credit or points for the number of entries of a particular sort. Some teachers collect informal writing from a fifth of the class each day, although I could never make that work. If you are working with portfolios, you might have a page in the portfolio in which students would discuss their own informal or expressive writing during the term, noting how they used it, how it helped them in their thinking, reading, and writing of more formal papers, and how it changed during the term.

One last note about journals: If you have structured a free-writing journal situation, you must be prepared for consequences. Think carefully about your responsibility to the student and the student's parents. In light of potential legal ramifications stemming from a journal entry, it may be advisable to set limits, such as telling students that this is a public, as opposed to a private journal; that it should contain no personal or family secrets; that it is serving a sound academic purpose, which is to improve writing. Some teachers prefer to set topics related to ideas generated by classroom reading or study. The important thing is to set a framework with which you and your students are comfortable.

Informative or Efferent Writing: "This is what I know and how I know it."

Informative writing presents what a writer knows about a subject in a way that communicates that knowledge effectively to a reader. It takes into account the needs of readers by putting the information into an appropriate context—orienting the reader, giving appropriate examples, disclosing background, and citing sources of information. Successful informative writers explain their ideas and elaborate information with sufficient detail to provide the reader with a clear understanding of the subject.

Informative writing provides readers with information about a subject or topic rather than persuading them to share a point of view or take any action. It focuses on a topic or subject rather than on the writer's private experience or attitude toward the subject. On the other hand, effective informative writing may use point of view and personal anecdote to reveal the writer as a knowledgeable source of information with a commitment to sharing this information with others. In its highly crafted form, informational writing encompasses both aesthetic and efferent purposes.

Teachers can build on young students' enthusiastic and natural propensity for looking things up by encouraging them to write down and share their findings. Students may communicate their knowledge orally, in writing, or by drawings.

Assessing informative writing

Students can help build a rubric for assessing informative writing once they understand the nature of this kind of writing. The characteristics that can be assessed are focus and coherence, presentation and elaboration, and style. Since this kind of writing has a specific audience, the use of conventions may also be the basis for a separate score. Suggested categories for constructing a rubric for informative writing follow.

Focus/Coherence
Direction: Writers develop a topic or controlling idea by presenting information and explanations in a purposeful way.

Organization: Writers establish a context for the presentation of their information; they arrange ideas and details in logical and useful ways, which help readers to understand the subject; their papers end with a sense of conclusiveness.

Presentation/Elaboration
Depth or Density of Information: Writers use a variety of strategies to present specific, detailed information, which may include anecdotes, the recounting of events, and elaborated descriptions.

Details: Writers choose appropriate details and elaborate them, using concrete language and sensory descriptions.

Audience: These writers meet the needs and expectations of readers for sufficiently detailed and relevant information on the topic; readers have a clear understanding of what the writer knows and how that knowledge was acquired.

Style
The writing has a sense of authority that reflects the writer's expertise in the subject. The tone may be informal or formal, but writers show confidence in their knowledge and enthusiasm about sharing it.

Persuasive Writing: "This is what I believe and why I think you should believe it."

Persuasive writing requires students to choose positions, state judgments or offer proposals, and to argue convincingly for their beliefs and ideas. Effective persuasive writers use reasons, evidence, examples, and/or anecdotes to support their arguments. Convincing arguments may appeal to logic, emotions, and/or philosophical beliefs.

Effective writers of persuasion establish themselves as informed, knowledgeable individuals. They orient readers by describing the subject, giving background information to focus the writing. More than any other kind of writing, persuasive writing requires writers to consider their audiences. Writers are aware of readers throughout the piece, perhaps referring to them directly, acknowledging their possible objections and reservations, or trying to enlist their support. The best writers of persuasion systematically develop arguments with a strong sense of coherence and movement. Such writers are, of course, interested in the craft of shaping their arguments and may combine persuasive and aesthetic purposes.

Teachers can build on students' strong opinions and natural propensity for arguing their points of view by encouraging them to present arguments orally in class as well as to write letters, editorials, and articles on controversial issues being discussed in class.

Assessing persuasive writing
Persuasive writing may be assessed by a rubric using the same categories as those for informational writing. The differences lie within the descriptions for each of these categories.

Focus/Coherence
Position: Writers usually assert and maintain a clear position throughout the piece; evidence and explanations are used to clarify, expand, or support this position.

Organization: Writers establish a context for the presentation of their ideas. Writers arrange details, reasons, examples, and/or anecdotes in an effective, persuasive way. The most effective papers often use an organization that is surprising or unusual.

Coherence: Papers are unified. Papers show effective cohesion—clear and smooth transitions between sequential sections of a paper, as well as overall coherence.

Elaboration
Support: Writers support their position with convincing reasons, examples, anecdotes, and/or information.

Depth/Density of Arguments: Writers thoroughly develop and elaborate one or more of their reasons, examples, anecdotes, and/or supportive information. They may use a variety of strategies to elaborate.

Audience: Writers choose and present arguments with a clear awareness of their audience. They show credibility and a sense of authority by revealing their sources of information. Effective papers usually anticipate and address reader misconceptions or counterarguments.

Style
Writers exhibit a strong voice that conveys a commitment to sharing their knowledge and point of view. They show confidence, conviction, and enthusiasm. Their language and sentence structure shows a careful attention to persuasive appeal.

Literary or Aesthetic Writing: "This is how I have shaped my ideas about what I have seen, experienced, or imagined."

Any writing growing out of the previous purposes may move into the aesthetic realm when the work is crafted into an art form such as story, poem, or essay. In this realm, the purpose of shaping ideas into a crafted piece works in concert with the purpose to reflect, inform, or persuade. Young children, if they are fortunate, grow up with stories and poems. In school, children hear, read, and write stories. By middle school, most students are familiar with the idea of telling a story, but few students at this age have learned how to craft a story. In response to one statewide assessment calling for eighth-grade students to write stories, for example, few students were able to do more than retell movies or stories that they had heard. The seventy middle school teachers reading and assessing the student papers concluded that although most middle school teachers asked students to write stories on particular occasions such as Halloween, they very rarely actually taught students how to write a story. In the following year, when teachers had incorporated the teaching of story writing into their programs, the quality of student stories improved markedly.

Narrative engages readers with a story line and enables them to enter the writer's real or imaginary world. Narrative writing is characterized by movement through time. It requires writers to establish a situation or setting; develop believable characters, either real or imagined; and tell what happened. Story writers use narrative strategies such as dialogue, description, sensory details, and concrete language as appropriate to create an event or experience for the reader. Narration is the primary mode for developing autobiographical incidents as well as fiction and is an important strategy used in other types of writing, such as biographical, informative, and persuasive writing.

Most elementary teachers take advantage of children's natural response to sound and rhythm to have them write poems as well as listen to them. Unfortunately, in too many intermediate and high school classes, little time is given to a serious study of the art of crafting poems. Such deprivation is a loss to our students and to our culture that we cannot afford. When given the opportunity, students discover that writing poems is a powerful medium for them; they often write compelling poems. The key is to begin with the students' purposes, then help them learn how to shape their ideas into appropriate forms. There are a number of useful resources for teaching students how to use established forms, such as the sonnet; to create their own forms, as Dylan Thomas did with his syllabics; or to let the form emerge organically, as in free verse. One reason that the writing of stories and poems is not taught as often as essay writing is that aesthetic or literary forms of writing are rarely included in assessment programs at any level. Many teachers, lacking a useful rubric, are uncomfortable assessing poems, for example, and are daunted by the prospect of "grading" a twelve-page story. School or district competency standards for writing rarely include stories and poems. Because assessment, whether we like it or not, drives curriculum, literary forms, although sometimes assigned, have not been included in the serious writing programs of too many classrooms. Encouraging all students to experience the joy of creating a carefully shaped piece of writing, whatever its form, leads to many of the values educators espouse—increased understanding of the power of language, enhanced self-esteem, and pride in one's accomplishments among them. The question then becomes, how can we design ways of assessing achievement in writing poetry and fiction as well as we do analytic, informative, and persuasive essays?

Assessing aesthetic or literary writing

It is impossible to design a rubric that extends to all forms of aesthetic or literary writing because nearly all kinds of writing may be elevated to that level. For informational and persuasive writing, for example, you would use the existing rubric but extend and elaborate on the style section, paying attention to precision of word choice, appropriateness of detail, and effectiveness of the overall presentation—the formal elements that show attention to craft as well as idea. It is difficult to separate these elements and may not even be advisable to do so except to help students focus on their ultimate purpose in writing. When the goal is persuasion, craft becomes a way to achieve the goal.

When assessing kinds of writing usually considered as "literary," we need to design rubrics that focus on specific genres. Here, I will present the characteristics that might be used to construct a rubric for narrative writing and make some comments about assessing poetry.

Assessing narrative writing

The effective narrative writer engages the reader by establishing a story situation and assuming a narrative stance or point of view at the outset. The writer develops the story through characterization and narrative strategies. These, then, will provide the categories from which to construct a rubric for the assessment of stories.

Situation
Writers establish the situation by setting the action of the story within a context so that readers understand the significance of the central action of the story. Setting and characters are firmly established. A conflict or tension is set early. The story then moves through a series of events or through character change to a logical resolution. The ending, on reflection by the reader, seems to be inevitable, even when it is surprising.

Characterization
Writers develop complex central characters rather than stereotypes. Some of the strategies used to develop characters are

- showing the character in action
- using dialogue to reveal how the character talks
- letting the reader "overhear" the character's inner thoughts

- reporting what other characters say about the character
- noting how others react to the actions or speech of the character
- telling readers directly about the character's appearance, personality, or behavior
- showing a character's emotional responses to situations
- revealing a character's relationships with other people
- presenting character changes or insights developed as a consequence of their actions
- Providing character motivation for behavior or decisions affecting the resolution of conflict or tension

Narrative strategies

Writers frame stories by the effective use of time and place. They establish a narrative stance or point of view; they pace their stories by balancing summary, dramatized incidents, and description. Writers order events in such a way as to control the movement of the story.

Strategies for pacing include

- straightforward chronology
- stream of consciousness
- episodes and transitions
- flashbacks
- foreshadowing
- withholding information to establish suspense

Use of concrete language and detail

Writers select the kinds of details that help readers imagine the sensory world in which the story occurs. Effective details are significant in rendering characters, in creating a believable fictional world, and in developing the story line. Details are precise and concrete and often developed by analogy or metaphor.

Unity

An effective story effectively unifies all of the narrative aspects; the story moves according to its internal rules, demonstrating a plausible logic with the story's context. The exceptional story has an interesting story line, believable characters, and strong supporting details, as well as an overall balance and stylistic unity.

Assessing poetry

Assessing student poetry requires a close knowledge of a student's experience with and expertise in writing poetry. In a class where students write poetry frequently and well, standards are considerably higher than in a class where students have scarcely read, much less written, a poem. There are a number of useful books for teachers to use in teaching students to write poetry, but little to help teachers evaluate what students are doing.

A caveat: Don't overpraise a student for a poem that is mediocre. Students won't believe you and furthermore won't know how to improve as poets. By responding to effective words, the use of concrete language and sensory details, or an original metaphor, one can encourage the student and point out characteristics that make effective poems. By far, the best teachers of poetry are poems themselves, as well as others who are writing and talking about their poems. A classroom in which books of poems are dog-eared and students share their poems can become a room in which young poets learn to appreciate and critique their own and each other's work. The key words are *image, action,* and *truth.* We might add, for Keats' benefit, *beauty.*

Secondary Writing Types

While the four global writing types are appropriate for all age groups, they can be refined as students gain expertise in the ability to handle the more specific demands of such writing types as evaluation, interpretation, and reflection. Table 3-1 shows how some commonly taught kinds of writing can be placed into the framework of the four basic writing categories. The school level indicates a rough estimate of when students might be developmentally ready to begin working with or focus on particular writing types. It is important to remember when looking at this grid that all types except the global expressive can reach the realm of aesthetic, depending on purpose and craft. A rubric can, of course, be developed for each of these types. A sample rubric that can be used in the classroom appears in Appendix Three.

The Uses of Writing

Understanding purpose in writing is basic to deciding how to use writing in the English classroom. It sounds almost ludicrous to write about "the uses of writing" in English classes: nearly everything we do involves writing. My aim here, however, is to ask you to look carefully at some of the uses we make of writing and consider whether we are *teaching* as well as *using* it as effectively as we might be.

Although Table 3-1 shows a number of specific writing types, each of which has particular features, it doesn't address the many

Table 3-1

TYPES OF WRITING	Primary	Middle School	High School
LITERARY or AESTHETIC		X	XXX
Story, poem, essay, dramatic work		X	XXX
EXPRESSIVE	XXX	X	X
Autobiographical incident		X	XX
Firsthand biographical sketch		XX	X
Reflections		X	XX
PERSUASIVE	X		
Problem solution essay		XX	XX
Evaluation essay		X	XX
Speculation essay		X	XX
Interpretative essay		X	XXX
Controversial issues essay		XX	XX
INFORMATIVE or EFFERENT	XX		
Report of information essay		XX	X
Observational writing		X	XX

uses we make of writing as integral to the processes involved in reading, writing that is done as part of research, writing as a way of studying, or the many other uses we make of writing throughout a school day. The more we learn about the way writing is tied to thinking, the more we find writing used in other disciplines—mathematics and science as well as history/social studies.

The section on expressive writing addressed some of the uses we make of writing in an informal way, but certainly not all; and it did not address how to assess writing that is undertaken chiefly for another purpose, such as reading or solving a problem in calculus. As has been emphasized throughout this chapter, the key word again is *purpose*. When the purpose is to take accurate notes for a science project, then the notes can be assessed for selectivity and accuracy. When the purpose is to write a letter to the editor of the local newspaper, the letter can be assessed according to whether it is intended to be informative or persuasive. A reading log should not be "corrected," but it can be assessed according to appropriate elements in the list of Reading Performances.

The reason for the emphasis on writing types in the first part of this chapter now becomes central. We can teach students to identify the characteristics of writing that they do for diverse reasons. They will see many overlaps, but they will also see some features that are emphasized in *persuasion*, perhaps, that are not important in *autobiographical incident*. The need for textual references in *interpretation* is not a hallmark of *reflection*. An essay may well combine interpretive and reflective elements; the criteria for assessing it may be adjusted accordingly. The emphasis on writing types is not to limit the teacher or student to working within these types as strict frameworks, but to use them as a guide to helping students see that different uses of writing require different emphases. It is easier to work from specific types than to begin with the hybrids that make up many of our day-to-day uses of writing.

The most effective way to teach students how to evaluate their work according to how well it achieves its purpose is to assign a carefully worded prompt that leads inevitably toward writing for a particular purpose, then have students work in teams, with their papers, to identify the features that make the writing successful. Working with the whole class, then, the teacher can distill the points made by individual teams and create a sound, workable rubric to be applied to that kind of writing. To illustrate this process, here are the features that characterize an evaluation, followed by a student paper and a sample response guide.[1]

Characteristics of Evaluation as a Writing Type

The writer of evaluation makes a judgment about a specific subject and supports, explains, or validates that judgment through the use of evidence. The writer must formulate or choose criteria on which to base the judgment. An awareness of audience determines what information to present about the subject and what biases or limitations to consider in addressing specific audiences. Voice and tone convey the writer's attitude toward the subject. The writer focuses the subject to be evaluated, orienting readers so that they can follow the argument.

Judgment

Evaluation requires a judgment based on the thoughtful examination of the subject. Implied or stated, the judgment makes an assertion about the subject's worth. Evaluation is more than the simple expression of likes and dislikes. Although personal preference may be a factor, evaluation depends on a critical assessment of the subject based on logically formulated criteria. The selection of criteria is crucial in that it often determines how effectively the judgment can be supported and may even determine what judgment is made.

Criteria

In drafting effective evaluations, writers identify criteria integral to the subject being evaluated. These criteria may focus on the subjects' importance or unique qualities. Often the writer chooses criteria that are traditionally and specifically associated with the subject. In a testing situation, students may be asked to evaluate the quality or appropriateness of a poem or short story by using criteria previously determined by the teacher, the class, or an external authority. In a self-determined work, however, the writer develops his or her own criteria.

The category of the subject helps the writer determine appropriate criteria. For instance, deciding which movie is more successful—*Star Wars* or *Grapes of Wrath*—depends on whether the writer selects "socially significant" or "technically innovative" or some other quality as the dominant feature of the movie. Choosing dramatic camera angles, startling special effects, and subtle editing leads to one judgment; choosing such criteria as accurate depiction of a problem, ability to influence attitudes, and power to bring about social change leads to another. The writer of a successful evaluation essay presents criteria clearly and applies them consistently in assessing the subject.

Evidence

Evaluation presents clearly stated, well-developed, and convincing evidence to support each judgment. A number of strategies, such as the following, are available to the writer:

- Analyze the subject.
- Compare and contrast subjects in the same category.

- Include personal experience or the experience of others.
- Cite authorities.
- Cite lines from a passage, literary work, movie, or song.
- Use observations of specimens, as in a study of plants or animals.
- Use notes of procedures in experiments.

Audience

Awareness of audience, which determines how much and what type of background information the writer must include, governs the strategies writers use in their evaluation and influences the tone of the essay. The writer of evaluation maintains a consistently authoritative tone. Although writers may entertain other points of view as they build their arguments, they always keep their own positions clear. The voice of most skillful writers is confident and committed; the writer's attitude toward the subject is explicit, evident, and consistent.

To orient and accommodate the reader to the subject, the writer may use a variety of strategies, such as the following:

- Set a framework for the evaluation, acknowledging the possible expertise and interest of the audience.
- Devise beginnings that acquaint readers with the subject.
- Describe the subject, its characteristics, and significance.
- Provide information the audience may not know.
- Describe personal experiences or feelings associated with the subject.
- Address possible audience concerns and questions.
- Direct some concluding remarks to the audience.

Exemplary Student Essay

The following essay was written by a high school junior who was asked to write an article evaluating a particular product for a consumer magazine. The article was to convince readers of the advantages or benefits of the product by establishing evaluative criteria and providing evidence of its worth. While the computer information may be somewhat dated, the characteristics of an evaluation are evident.

Love at First Mini-Byte

I'm having an intimate relationship with my computer. Nestled in my lap, my lean, compact Zenith-181 invites opening. A lifting of the hinged lid uncovers a pristine keyboard and reveals a dark window in the lid. Power on, and the window turns a lustrous pearl grey on which reassuring blue letters glow. In a dark room its effect is aqueous, like watching luminescent tropical fish glide by in a deep sea vault, ever so comforting, ever so gentle on the eyes.

Lest you think I am developing an as-yet-undefined but nonetheless perverted Freudian relationship with my computer, let me explain my affinity. I own a personal computer, and it serves me well. But it is not mobile. Unless you call hauling a computer in my Volkswagen "mobile." A few years ago "portables" emerged on the scene. They resemble small movie projectors, and well-muscled business executives lug them around. Then along came the Z-181 and its compatriots, so-called "laptop" computers. These elfin wonders with one-fifth the size but more than twice the memory of their desktop cousins of a year ago, have another advantage over their peers: they're cute. I can kiss mine for writing an "A" essay, clutch it to my chest for comfort and consolation, or swing it with careless abandon as I skip joyously to school. It is my companion. More than simply personal, it's as intimate as my toothbrush, a confidential partner, at my side, on my mind, under my fingertips.

But cooler sorts are convinced by data. Here come some, straight from the manual: 640K memory; two 3.5 inch disk drives, each storing 720K (twice the storage of a normal PC); running speed of 4.77 megahertz; interfaces with external 5.25 disk drive; fully MS-DOS compatible; AC converter/recharger; weight a little over eleven pounds; cost $2000, a price tag only the son of a generous president of a computer company can afford. But the price, as with most computers, will decrease in time.

Software for laptop computers is a major problem, but not an insurmountable one. Most MS-DOS programs exists on 5.25 floppies, not 3.5 inch disks. But many fully equipped computer stores will transfer MS-DOS software from 5.25 inch to 3.5 inch formats. Also, if you already own a PC, you can buy a program called The Brooklyn Bridge, link your PC and laptop to create one machine with four disk drives, and transfer files from 5.25 to 3.5 inch or vice versa.

Although laptops are marketed as executive accessories, the Z-181 is a perfect introduction for a computer neophyte. Its resemblance to a portable typewriter with a lid reassures the uninitiated threatened by more massive equipment. It requires no assembly; batteries are included. Just open it up, switch it on, and away you go. The small screen looks just like Etch a Sketch, as one of my friends said. And it does, except it can do so much more than just duplicate doodles.

Data General and NEC produce fine laptop computers, but the Toshiba T1100 Plus is probably the most popular. Their more recent model, the T3100, is a powerhouse laptop for big boys and girls who do more than duplicate doodlings or write essays, who probably crush atoms or crunch conglomerates for a living.

I prefer the Z-181 over other models for several reasons. Primo, my generous president of a computer company father gave it to me. Segundo, that luminescent, easy-on-the-eyes screen. Most laptops have screen displays of liquid crystal, like a calculator's, visible only in good light. The Z-181 glows legibly even in near-dark. It's because of something called a "backlit supertwisted birefringent screen" which sounds like two tortured Amanas to me. Whatever it is, it makes for easy viewing. Additionally, the Z-181 does not suffer from the malady of many laptops; squashed screen displays producing the fun-house mirror effect of stunted, squat shapes. The Z-181 screen produces the same proportions as my desktop PC, so the only distortions of reality appear in my mind, not on the screen.

In this post-transistor, microchip world, small is beautiful and portable is progress. In the movie *Peggy Sue Got Married*, Peggy Sue through her 1950's eyes foresees that "In the future, everything gets smaller, except portable radios." Even the ghetto-blaster may give way to the Walkman and to the compact disc player. Twenty years ago a computer was as large as a room; now it can sit on a child's lap (if it wants to). Sometime soon I suspect we'll have a stamp-sized computer used by Lilliputians. "Think small" will be our motto. I'm taking shrinking lessons now.

Before this student submitted this article, he wrote a rough draft, made a graphic with a slogan to accompany the article (a drawing of an elf with a computer working on the lap of a large figure, seen only in the two legs forming a lap; its caption is "A little love begins in a lap—make it yours."), and filled out a revision guide. The revision guide was specific to the assignment; all students could use it. Its main emphasis was to have students identify where in their articles they had met the criteria for good evaluations. They worked with partners to plan revisions.

A response and revision guide that is more generically useful for evaluation essays follows. It can be used by individuals or writing partners to plan revision strategies.

Response and Revision

Use the following questions as you discuss your drafts:

Audience's knowledge of the subject
- How much knowledge of the subject does the reader have?
- What kinds of information will I need to supply so that the reader will accept my evaluation?

Criteria
- Are my criteria appropriate to the subject I am evaluating?
- What further evidence do I need to strengthen my evaluation?

Organization
- How should I capture my reader's attention at the beginning of my article?
- How can I sequence my reasons so that they effectively support my judgment?
- What is irrelevant or ineffective in my article and could be deleted?
- How should I end my essay—by summarizing my reasons, by restating my judgment, or by using some other strategy?

Student responses need to be thoughtful, helpful, and specific. The purpose of responding to another student's paper is to assist the writer during the revision process—to provide suggestions for the writer to use in rethinking or reseeing his or her essay. A workshop guide must not be seen by the writer as a list of instructions to be followed during the revision process. The writer needs to maintain ownership of his or her paper, selecting and discarding advice as appropriate to the purpose of the paper. The response guide can provide the author with a sound beginning toward revision, which we teach as part of the ongoing process of self-assessment.

Just as the governing principle in teaching writing is to build on author purpose, so the controlling factor in assessment is to appraise the degree to which the writer has achieved his or her purpose. A natural extension of thought leads to the premise that knowledgeable self-assessment is the most valid measure we have of whether the writer has achieved his or her purpose. In order to have an accurate self-assessment, students must be secure in the belief that they can determine their success as writers. Such belief, however, is not inborn or transmitted through overtly working on increasing self-esteem. On the contrary, self-esteem rises when students understand the criteria by which their work is to be measured and learn to apply it to their own writing.

Chapter Four

Structuring and Assessing Integrated Projects

The thing that distinguishes a unit from a project is the way we conceptualize their purposes. In a *unit,* the focus is usually on the material to be covered. In a *project,* the focus is on the activity of a team of students working together toward a common goal. A unit may include a number of assignments, including one or more projects; or it may be construed as a single project. Using the concept of teams rather than groups helps convey the importance of working together toward a specific end. The *team* approach is an increasingly significant one in the world of work, where many companies are structuring their employees to work as teams, giving them specific goals for specific projects. Most teachers have, of course, long ago incorporated *group* work into their learning strategies, but many are still uncertain as to how to structure such groups for maximum collaborative productiveness; still more are finding that the difficulties of assessing such group work sometimes are greater than the rewards. In schools where teachers have worked together to solve these problems, the rewards are astounding. In any event, the necessity for schools to shift their thinking from the early twentieth-century individualized approach to learning, where talking was minimal and working together a suspect arrangement, to a design that includes both individual and team-oriented activities becomes more and more apparent as our society moves toward project-oriented businesses, manufacturers, and service organizations.

Literature-Based Projects

Reading, talking, and writing about literature has long been the mainstay of the English classroom. A love of literature is what brought most of us into the profession. And although it is true that we have come to see many other aspects of language learning as our responsibility, often even our primary responsibility, we continue to use literature as the springboard for activities in our classrooms. It is natural, then, that many, if not most, of our teaching units are based on literature, either single works or clustered groups of pieces related by genre or by theme. Even projects that set out with non-literary goals, such as the I-Search paper or the interview, usually have a literature component. When such units are conceived as projects, or contain small projects within them, students work together in teams to read, write, draw, interview, videotape, conduct research in libraries through the Internet, and, most of all, talk with each other about what they are discovering; in this kind of learning environment, the question of assessment becomes even more baffling than it is in a more traditional classroom. How to handle the logistics, simply keeping track of what everyone is doing and how well they are doing it, can be a nightmare. Questions arise: Do we assess the individual or the group? How do we account for the uneven contributions that each member of the team makes? Do we assess steps in the process or just a finished product? Do we always include a written product or can the outcome of a project be a graphic, a film, a dance, a performance? Assessing what our students are actually learning has long been buried under how well they are able to write, how well they are able to express their ideas in the traditional essay format. Teaching English has been synonymous, not only in the eyes of outsiders, with correcting papers. It is no longer possible to conceive of our subject in this way.

In this chapter, I will present some possible answers to these questions. To lay the groundwork, I will present, first, an assignment that has both individual and team components. In this approach, the focus shifts back and forth from individual to team as students explore a single piece of literature from several angles of vision. This example displays multiple options for the study of a piece of literature. Rarely would we engage students in all of these activities for a single work; it is useful to take students through the entire process once, however, to introduce them to the possibilities that they will then be able to choose for themselves in subsequent, larger, team projects.

Designing a Task: Reading, Talking, and Writing about a Piece of Literature

For this task, students will read Margaret Atwood's short prose piece "Bread." They will look at it from different angles as they engage in the processes of constructing meaning. Some of these angles involve reading other pieces to extend their thinking beyond the core text. Students will work both individually and in groups as they read, talk, draw, and write. The questions and activities, although familiar kinds of experiences in many English classrooms, are intentionally grouped here to create multiple opportunities for students to engage in thinking about a text. They are also designed to enable both you and students to measure the depth of each student's reading and writing performance. The process of assessment will be both concurrent and summative. You will notice that many of the activities ask students to be reflective, preparing them for a more formal self-evaluation.

To work through these angles, have each student set up a log. Arrange the class in teams of three or four for sharing and collaborating. For some angles, several options are provided. Rarely would you want to assign all of these options to any one student, but by portioning out sections to different groups, then having them share their work, you can enable students to experience both breadth and depth in their study.

In setting up a sustained project, it is important to give students a sense of the whole. Let them know what kinds of activities they will be doing, how long the project will take, and how they will be assessed. Remember to stress to students that there is no *one way* or *right way* to interpret a piece of literature, but that they must account for their interpretation. As they talk and write, responding to different questions and activities, their ideas will grow and change. They'll keep a log of all of their responses so that they can see how their ideas grow as they make connections between ideas in the text, things that they have thought about from their own life, and ideas they've gotten from other sources such as books, movies, and observation. They will also read several additional pieces that they can relate to the central work.

Because one of the goals of this task is to have students monitor their own thinking, they should know in advance what sorts of things provide evidence of how they think as they read, write, and talk. Let students know that they should demonstrate that they can accomplish most of the following performance standards:

- construct a meaning that accounts for the whole text
- connect the ideas in the core work to other texts they will read as well as to their own experience, observations, or other art forms
- reflect on and explain what the text means to them
- extend their understanding of this text by discussing it with their team
- explore their own ideas on related topics through graphics, discussion, writing, and perhaps through other forms such as dance or film
- carry at least one piece of writing through to its finished state
- write a reflective self-evaluation of their work throughout the project

Students will be able to track their performances by keeping their responses in a folder that will form the basis for their portfolio work. When students review their achievement on this task, they will look at all of their work before they make a final self-evaluation.

Prereading Activities

While you may wish to make the reading of the text the initial activity, there are several prereading possibilities that have worked well in setting up this project.

Optional Activity 1

Bring to class several loaves of bread, one or two freshly baked baguettes, perhaps, or whole grain, and one typical supermarket loaf of sliced white bread. Ask the class to study the loaves and focus on their responses to the different breads. Have them record any memories or associations they have as they study the bread. After a few minutes of journal writing, ask them to get into teams and share the bread. This should be a self-conscious activity. They should monitor their own behavior as they decide which bread they want to share and how they make that decision. Think about how the teams are to be formed. If you leave the process to them, notice whether they select their teams first, probably on the basis of friendships in the class, or whether they gravitate toward their favorite type of bread and make up groups that share their taste. After they "break bread together," ask them to make further notes in their logs, including any additional associations or memories that were stimulated by eating the bread.

Optional Activity 2

Whenever you introduce Atwood's piece "Bread," there will undoubtedly be tragic stories of hunger and starvation in the news. Somalia and Bosnia-Hercegovina remain as testimony to the extreme deprivation people have suffered in some parts of a world when there is grain rotting in silos in another. Bring pictures and/or articles from newspapers or magazines; gather slides or videotapes from the library. Find an appropriate CD-ROM disk. Without much by way of commentary, share these materials. If you teach in a school where hunger is known, use local stories. If you teach in an affluent neighborhood, use stories from urban areas close by as well as those from other countries. Have students record their responses in their logs.

Optional Activity 3 (If you use this option, omit the student section "Getting Started.")

Pass out copies of "Bread" to the whole class. Read it aloud. You may want to have the class read it together in a choral reading. After the reading, ask each student to write down one word that expresses his or her immediate response. Go around the room and ask each person to read that word. There should be no interruptions or comments. Duplications are fine; they just reinforce the solidity of the class. This activity should be followed immediately by a log entry in which students write their initial responses more fully, preferably before discussion has blunted the edges of the initial effect of the piece.

Getting Started

Tell students they're going to read a short prose piece by Margaret Atwood entitled "Bread." As they read, they may write their thoughts, feelings, or questions in their logs or on Post-its that they can put in the margins. If they have their own copy of the text, they may write directly on it. They should have their logs handy so that they can record their first responses right after reading. Here is the piece:

Bread

by Margaret Atwood

Imagine a piece of bread. You don't have to imagine it, it's right here in the kitchen, on the breadboard, in its plastic bag, lying beside the bread knife. The bread knife is an old one you picked up at an auction; it has the word BREAD carved into the wooden handle. You

open the bag, pull back the wrapper, cut yourself a slice. You put butter on it, then peanut butter, then honey, and you fold it over. Some of
the honey runs out onto your fingers and you lick it off. It takes you
about a minute to eat the bread. This bread happens to be brown, but
there is also white bread, in the refrigerator, and a heel of rye you got
last week, round as a full stomach then, now going moldy. Occasionally you make bread. You think of it as something relaxing to do with
your hands.

Imagine a famine. Now imagine a piece of bread. Both of these
things are real but you happen to be in the same room with only one of
them. Put yourself into a different room, that's what the mind is for.
You are now lying on a thin mattress in a hot room. The walls are
made of dried earth, and your sister, who is younger than you, is in the
room with you. She is starving, her belly is bloated, flies land on her
eyes; you brush them off with your hand. You have a cloth too, filthy
but damp, and you press it to her lips and forehead. The piece of
bread is the bread you've been saving, for days it seems. You are as
hungry as she is, but not yet as weak. How long does this take? When
will someone come with more bread? You think of going out to see if
you might find something that could be eaten, but outside the streets
are infested with scavengers and the stink of corpses is everywhere.

Should you share the bread or give the whole piece to your sister?
Should you eat the piece of bread yourself? After all, you have a better
chance of living, you're stronger. How long does it take to decide?

Imagine a prison. There is something you know that you have not
yet told. Those in control of the prison know that you know. So do
those not in control. If you tell, thirty or forty or a hundred of your
friends, your comrades, will be caught and will die. If you refuse to
tell, tonight will be like last night. They always choose the night. You
don't think about the night however, but about the piece of bread they
offered you. How long does it take? The piece of bread was brown
and fresh and reminded you of sunlight falling across a wooden floor.
It reminded you of a bowl, a yellow bowl that was once in your home.
It held apples and pears; it stood on a table you can also remember.
It's not the hunger or the pain that is killing you but the absence of the
yellow bowl. If you could only hold the bowl in your hands, right here,
you could withstand anything, you tell yourself. The bread they offered
you is subversive, it's treacherous, it does not mean life.

There were once two sisters. One was rich and had no children,
the other had five children and was a widow, so poor that she no
longer had any food left. She went to her sister and asked her for a
mouthful of bread. "My children are dying," she said. The rich sister
said, "I do not have enough for myself," and drove her away from the

door. Then the husband of the rich sister came home and wanted to cut himself a piece of bread, but when he made the first cut, out flowed red blood.

Everyone knew what that meant.

This is a traditional German fairy tale.

The loaf of bread I have conjured for you floats about a foot above your kitchen table. The table is normal, there are no trap doors in it. A blue tea towel floats beneath the bread, and there are no strings attaching the cloth to the bread or the bread to the ceiling or the table to the cloth, you've proved it by passing your hand above and below. You didn't touch the bread though. What stopped you? You don't want to know whether the bread is real or whether it's just a hallucination I've somehow duped you into seeing. There's no doubt that you can see the bread, you can even smell it, it smells like yeast, and it looks solid enough, solid as your own arm. But can you trust it? Can you eat it? You don't want to know, imagine that.

Angle I: Initial Response

Log Entry: Ask students to *imagine bread.* Ask them to think about the words of this piece as they pertain to *bread.* What are their thoughts, feelings, observations, or questions after reading this piece? Have them use their logs to express their initial responses. They may use drawings as well as words.

In team discussion, they can share what they have written or drawn, then record in their logs any thoughts or questions that were stimulated by the discussion.

Angle II: Jigsaw Pieces

The task for this angle of vision is to have each team represent one section of the text graphically. Before you begin Angle II, divide a large piece of butcher paper into five puzzle pieces, each one large enough for a team graphic. Have enough colored markers for five teams. Divide the class into five teams and assign each team one of the five sections of "Bread." Ask students to read their assigned section of "Bread" silently. Before talking, they should write in their logs to answer questions such as these:

1. What puzzles you about this piece? Underline some of the puzzling phrases and/or images.
2. What image or images stand out for you?
3. What feelings does this section leave with you?
4. What questions do you have about this part?

In discussion, students might read some of their responses aloud as they explore what their section means and how they are going to represent that meaning on their piece of the puzzle. Then, using images, symbols, and words, students design a graphic to convey their interpretation of that section in light of the whole piece.

Class presentation is a critical aspect of this angle. When all groups are finished, someone from each team should read their section then place their puzzle piece on the wall. The team should explain their symbols and images and talk about what this section means in the context of the whole piece. The team presenting should lead the class in discussion. As the pieces begin to form the whole, discussion will become increasingly more productive.

Angle III: Shifting Perspectives

In Angle III, you'll ask students to shift their perspectives and imagine some other ways of looking at "Bread." Before beginning this section, rearrange the teams so that each new team contains one member of the five original teams. The new teams thus have one member who has dealt deeply with each section.

Ask students to skim the whole piece again and look at how their perspective shifts with each new section. Have them think about how successful Atwood was in moving them into the different scenes. Ask them which scene was the most vivid? Have them sketch this scene in their logs, then jot down their responses to these two questions.

1. What is it about the text itself that made this scene the most vivid for you?
2. What is it about *you* that made this scene vivid for you?

Ask students to share their responses with their team and determine whether their answers were more alike on question #1 or #2. Have them talk about the similarities and differences in their responses.

One of the ways to shift perspectives about a piece of literature is to play "what if?" and speculate about alternatives. For example, in focusing on the meaning of the title, students might consider how different titles would change the meaning of the text for them. Speculating on "what if" leads them back to "what is." Ask students to consider what other title might fit this text and how such titles would affect their interpretations. You might take a poll to find out what title, other than *Bread*, has the most provocative possibilities of interpretation. Students might finish this angle with a log entry on their understanding of how shifting their perspective affects their interpretation.

Angle IV: Connecting with the Writer

When we read, we bring our whole being into the transaction between us and the words on the page. Who we are, which includes where we have lived, the people we have known, the experiences we have had—all these things affect the meaning that we make as we read words on a page. Ask students to notice how they and other members of their team bring different perspectives to the reading of "Bread." When we know something about the author, that affects our reading, too. Margaret Atwood's personal and cultural history has infused this text with a very particular angle of vision. In this case, knowing that Margaret Atwood is Canadian and grew up in a country where survival was a way of life could affect the meaning it has for us.

Have students read the short biographical sketch and the extract from an article Atwood wrote about how basic survival is to Canadians.

Biographical Sketch

Margaret Atwood (1939–) has been a cashier and a filmscript writer, an editor with one of Canada's largest presses, and a professor of English literature. Born in Ottawa, Ontario, Atwood began writing as a child. Recently relating her love for domestic life to her literary career, Atwood claimed that "if Shakespeare could have kids and avoid suicide" then so could she. The fiction she produces ranges from serious probing into the psychological effects of modern culture to light and humorous stories. *The Handmaid's Tale* is among her novels.

Carving Out a Place and a Way of Keeping Alive

The central symbol for Canada—and this is based on numerous instances of its occurrence in both English and French Canadian literature—is undoubtedly Survival, *la Survivance* . . . Like the Frontier and The Island, it is a multi-faceted and adaptable idea. For early explorers and settlers, it meant bare survival in the face of "hostile" elements and/or natives; carving out a place and a way of keeping alive. But the word can also suggest survival of a crisis or disaster, like a hurricane or a wreck, and many Canadian poems have this kind of survival as a theme; what they might call *grim* survival as opposed to *bare* survival. For French Canada after the English took over it became cultural survival, hanging on as a people, retaining a religion and a language under an alien government. And in English Canada now while the Americans are taking over it is acquiring a similar meaning. There is another use of the word as well: a survival can be a vestige of a vanished order which has managed to persist after its time is past, like a primitive reptile. This version crops up in Canadian thinking too, usually among those who believe that Canada is obsolete.

But the main idea is the first one: hanging on, staying alive. Canadians are forever taking the national pulse like doctors at a sickbed: the aim is not to see whether the patient will live well but simply whether he will live at all. Our central idea is one which generates, not the excitement and sense of adventure or danger which The Frontier holds out, not the smugness and/or sense of security, of everything in its place, which The Island can offer, but an almost intolerable anxiety. Our stories are likely to be tales not of those who made it but of those who made it back, from the awful experience—the North, the snowstorm, the sinking ship—that killed everyone else. The survivor has no triumph or victory but the fact of his survival; he has little after his ordeal that he did not have before, except gratitude for having escaped with his life.

In team discussion, have students talk about whether the survival theme that Atwood sees as characteristic of the Canadian people is reflected in "Bread." Then ask them to explore in their logs how their understanding of "Bread" has been affected by this added information and by their discussion.

Angle V: Language and Craft

The line between prose and poetry is a loose one. Atwood, as both a novelist and a poet, often blurs the distinction in her short pieces such as "Bread." One of the *poetic* aspects of "Bread" is her strong use of visual images.

Students can talk with their team about the sequence of images in this piece. Ask them to look again at their jigsaw graphics and notice what images they selected to record in each section. Have them select the visual image in the total work that they found the strongest and sketch it in their logs. Then, using a dual-entry format (two columns), have them jot down in Column One the words and phrases that create this image for them. In Column Two, they should explain how each word or phrase affects the way they visualize and interpret this piece.

In groups, have students reread the text and talk about any other poetic qualities it has. For instance, how do the repetitions within sections or at the ends of sections affect their reading of it? Is this piece a poem? A short story? Talk about how they would classify it, but remind them that there are no right answers to this question. The important thing is to back up their opinion with reasonable explanations. Ask students whether knowing the form of a text helps them in any way as they read and think about it.

Have students record in their logs the essence of their discussions with their team and with the class about form and about how the form of a work affects their understanding or enjoyment. Invite them to draw heavily on other works they have read as they think through this question.

Angle VI: Recasting the Text

Literature is filled with what we call *recastings*. These recastings may take many forms: Writers may retell the original so that a story takes place in a different time period with different kinds of people or they may change the form of the original—from a story to a play, for example, or from a painting to a poem. You might brainstorm recastings that are part of the popular culture: How many versions are there of Romeo and Juliet, for example?

Have students try recasting "Bread" in any of these ways, or in other ways of their own:

- as a series of drawings
- as a poem
- as a serious cartoon strip, with appropriate captions for each block
- as a letter from a person who is in prison to a member of his/her family
- as a report from a worker in a homeless shelter who is trying to convince local restaurants to contribute food to the shelter

Ask students to share their work with their team. You may also wish to have them share with other members of the class.

Angle VII: You, the Text, the World

We hope that this approach to "Bread" has helped students see different ways they, as readers, can learn more, not only about the text they are reading, but also about their own ways of constructing meaning from their transactions with events in their life. Reading is one kind of event that helps shape who we are as human beings. As students continue to work and play with the meaning of texts, they will find that they use some of these angles or lenses more often than others; they may find that one angle is appropriate to a story and another angle is more useful with an essay, while still another is appropriate to the way they "read" the behavior of a friend.

It is important for students to know that they do not need to come to a final conclusion about the meaning of a work of literature. They may need to form their ideas about the meaning a work has for them at a particular moment, for an immediate purpose; another day, however, when they are in a different mood or have had an experience that relates to the events in a story, they may find their understanding or envisionment of the story has changed.

Every step they take toward creating richer meaning involves changing perspectives, making connections, and facing new possibilities. They make interpretive decisions each time they look through a different lens. By looking at a work from different angles, they will find their reading of books as well as of life becomes more imaginative, intellectual, and finely tuned.

Ask students to read through their logs and think about the various activities they've done with Margaret Atwood's text "Bread." They can talk with their team about how their understanding and appreciation of the text has changed or deepened as they have looked at it from different angles, as they have talked, written, and drawn their ideas. You might ask:

- What new questions can they ask now?
- Which angles of vision gave them the most insight and the most pleasure as they worked with this text?
- What else can they say about the meaning of this text?

Using their logs, the text, their own responses, and events in their own experience that they feel are relevant, ask students to write and/ or draw their reflections about the meaning this text has for them now.

Writing a Piece for their Portfolio

As students reread the logs they wrote about "Bread" for each of the lenses or angles of vision, they can think about what ideas they would like to work with for a finished piece. Once they have decided on an idea that they want to develop, they can do some clustering or brainstorming to generate additional ideas. Here is what they've already done:

As they worked through the various approaches to this one text, they

- recorded their thoughts and feelings
- looked at parallel stories from other texts, art forms, or their own experience
- speculated on how their reading might change if they changed various aspects of the text
- noted how additional information about Atwood affected their reading

- looked at how the form of the text figured into their understanding
- recast the text in different ways
- reflected on which angles of vision were important or useful for understanding and appreciating the text.

As they consider their proposed portfolio piece, they need to think about two aspects of their proposed product, as each will affect the other: the nature of the idea they want to develop and the form or forms they want to use to develop that idea. Here are some options that work with texts such as "Bread."

Written options

1. Write a dialogue with the author, section by section.
2. Write a prose piece like Atwood's using a different familiar concrete object instead of bread. Begin some paragraphs with the word *imagine.*
3. Write a poem: Turn "Bread" or another of the pieces they read into a poem, perhaps modeling it on another poem they have read this year.
4. Write a paper about Margaret Atwood, based on additional readings of her poetry or fiction.
5. Look at the contrasts and clashes of realities they have discovered and discussed in "Bread" and other works. Write an essay in which they reflect upon one of the more significant contradictions of our times. Show how two realities concerning the same issue exist in a state of conflict. Relate their ideas about this contradiction in terms of their own life. Explore their thoughts and feelings about this paradox, ponder its significance, its impact on their life. What does this conflict say about who we are as people? What are the universal implications of this existing state of tension? Try to discover some *universal truth* about living in a state of contrast, paradox, and absurdity.

Graphic options

Students do not need to have artistic ability to begin working with graphics; their goal is to translate their ideas into symbols and images, using both drawings and words as they are appropriate. They are not simply *illustrating* the work; they are showing how they understand the work through metaphor and symbol. Students probably have the origin for a portfolio graphic in their logs; have them look through the logs to get ideas for how they might develop ideas that were stimulated by their work in this unit. Graphic options may stand alone or may accompany a written option. If the graphic stands alone, students should write a short explanation of the piece for their portfolio.

For graphics, students will need paper, marking pens, crayons, or watercolors. Here are some suggestions they may use to stimulate their own ideas:

1. Map the parallels between "Bread" and another work they have read.
2. Create a sun-shadow mandala for a loaf of bread. (See Appendix One for instructions on creating the sun-shadow mandala.)
3. Decide on an abstraction that underlies "Bread." Students might use the idea of clashing realities as in the previous "Written Options" section or *hunger* or *loss of freedom* as the basis for a sun-shadow mandala.
4. Create a map or mandala for the *I* of "Bread," the narrator who asks them to "Imagine bread."

Performance options
Performance options may include written work and graphics as well as performances, if they are part of the presentation. Students may want to work with a partner or a small team to prepare a dramatic performance; they may, of course, design a solo presentation.

Suggestions:

1. With a partner, have students plan "freeze frames" for significant points in each section. They should plan how they will physically represent the characters that they invent at each point. What facial expression will they have? What gestures? What stance—standing, kneeling, bent over? Have them polish their performance for the class. One student should read the text aloud as the performers present their interpretation, moving from frame to frame.
2. Have students look back at the logs for story threads, shifting perspectives, and ways of recasting the text. Working in groups of two or three, have students prepare a storytelling session, with all of their stories related in some way to the vignettes presented in "Bread." By listening to each other, they can refine their stories before presenting them to the class.
3. Working with a partner or team, students can compose music and/ or choreograph a dance to depict the changing scenes in "Bread."

From Process to Product

So much has been written about the importance of *process* in contemporary pedagogy that some teachers have neglected teaching students how to conceptualize, design, revise, and publish a *product*. In a product-oriented society, we would not be serving our students well if we omitted giving them the experience of carrying a project through to a refined, finished product. The personal sense of accomplishment that such an endeavor engenders makes it even more important to devote time to the actual teaching of rather than just assigning a final product in a project. The success of a final product—written, graphic, oral presentation, a combination—depends on the ability to see something through to completion. There are several factors that will help students learn how they work best and how they can take advantage of that knowledge as they develop an idea into its best possible form.

Steps in Working through a Major Paper or Project

Step 1: Messing around

Students need to learn the value of the "messing around" stage. Often this stage will begin in their log entries. In order to find out exactly what they want to do, however, they need to be able to make a number of starts, often in different directions. The teacher's role in this stage is critical; as teacher, you can suggest possibilities that are not within their realm of a student's experience. Suggesting that a talented singer compose her own music for her poetry may provide the inspiration for a new slant to her future. Suggesting that students organize an investigation into the way their community deals with the homeless and hungry might result in a deepened level of awareness about social programs.

During this stage, students should be taught to pay attention to the ways that they learn, that they process information or engage in critical/creative activities. They need information about how the brain works and how their brains work best as they explore their own ways to get started, whether it is through talking, reading, clustering, mapping, listing, brainstorming, or just free-writing their way into a topic. Although this stage is often glibly referred to as "prewriting," that term is a misnomer; the "messing around" stage is vital to critical, creative thinking and students may return to this stage a number of times during the course of completing their project.

Step 2: Making a rough draft, notes, sketches

Once students have decided on their ideas, they need to establish a space in which to work. Even in the classroom, surrounded by other teams that may be talking, they can cultivate their own space in which to write or draw.Students who elect to work on a team project must keep careful notes as to what each member of the group contributes. (See forms at the end of this chapter.) In their first draft, they try to develop their ideas as fully as they can in a relatively short period of time, depending on the scope of their planned work. When they have their ideas roughly sketched out, they can begin the refining, re-visioning process. This is the point where form becomes a critical issue.

Step 3: Collaborating, sharing with their team

Although group brainstorming can be fruitful, the real value of collaboration begins after students have their first ideas drafted. This is the time for writing response teams, for sharing their work and getting feedback from others. Since they are the ones who know what their goals are, they are the ones who must take the lead in telling their partners what they want from them. Sometimes they may just want to have them listen. Other times they may want specific revision suggestions. They can learn to use their best knowledge of what they need from their team and be sure to give back to the others what they ask for.

Step 4: Re-visioning

Again, after the collaboration, they will need a quiet time while they further revise and refine. Regardless of the help others may offer, each word or placement of design is ultimately their decision. They will take both the praise and the criticism. This part of the process is often the most satisfying—when they see their product really taking shape and becoming more than they even dreamed of in the beginning.

Step 5: Editing

In the case of a written work, this is the final step before publication. Here they may need the help of a partner; they may need to consult a dictionary or writing handbook. If they are using a word processor, they should be sure to use the spell check but be reminded that it does not catch a lot of typographical errors, *on* for *one,* for instance. They need to proofread carefully and, if possible, get someone else to proofread for them. (Not because they wouldn't recognize a typo, but because the eye sees what the brain expects.)

Step 6: Publication
This is the next-to-the-last step. For classroom projects, publication may take many forms. Finished written projects go into their portfolio, the collection of work they consider ready for publication. Finished graphics should be accompanied by a presentation to the class and go up on the wall of the classroom. Finished performances may be presented to other classes as well as their own. Several students may plan to take their performance "on the road," presenting it for their school open house, a PTA meeting, or an elementary school assembly. (My students say that children are often their best audiences!) For finished work that cannot go into the portfolio, they should write a short, concise explanation of the graphic or oral performance that they did for their project. Include the unit title, the assignment that they chose or their teacher construed, and a description of the finished work.

Step 7: Evaluating or assessing their finished product
Although you will be evaluating both finished products and student work throughout the process, a student's self-evaluation is an important key to his or her growth as a self-sufficient reader, writer, graphic artist, photographer, or performer. Before students can step back and reflect on their accomplishments usefully, they need to think through what their goals were in the beginning, how they changed as they worked, and how their final products reflect their thinking. As a final self-evaluation, ask students to write a brief assessment of their final product, stating:

1. what they hoped to accomplish when they began and
2. how their final work measures up to or differs from (falls below, exceeds) their expectations

Assessing the Student's Performance on the Task

Assume that my junior class has just completed a task similar to the one described. I am a conscientious teacher but have not had an opportunity to learn much about new theories of reading. I have heard the phrase *authentic assessment* but do not know how assessment could be any more authentic than it is in my class.

The task itself would not be quite the same as the description you have read: First of all, there would be significant omissions. The students would not have, up front, criteria for the eventual assessment of their work. The sections detailing self-assessment would be sketchy if they appeared at all. But assume that the task is roughly the same. What might my grade book look like? How would

I assess such an unwieldy task, made up of reading, discussion, writing, drawing, performing—all the diverse elements of English Language Arts? Here is a model with which most of us are familiar.

A familiar model of evaluating student achievement. Assuming that I am using the student grading paradigm with which most of us are familiar, I would keep a record of each aspect of the task as it is completed and mark down an idiosyncratic notation indicating the degree of completion: a check, check-minus, or check-plus. Completing the minitask is enough for credit. *Effort* is generally a key indicator for this mark. I would include a grade for a category called *participation*, based on my intuitive reading of the student's inter-action with other students. This, too, is part of the check system. Final projects would be graded primarily for effort, sometimes for ingenuity or creativity; since a letter grade is difficult to attach to effort or creativity, this grade seems arbitrary and I feel uncomfortable assigning it. The *real grade* for the task, however, is reserved for my evaluation of the required final paper.

Note that in the task as presented, the final projects were not proscribed; they were suggested. Students might or might not opt to do a final paper unless the teacher made it a requirement. But how can we give this unwieldy task a grade without it? As a teacher using this model, I would definitely assign a final paper; I would then go home for several nights with an armload of papers to "correct."

There would be a wide disparity among teachers in correcting or grading these papers, even those using this model. Some teachers would, in fact, "correct" the errors in conventions—spelling, mechanics, and usage—while others would be more likely to attend to the structure of the whole paper. Some would write a phrase or perhaps a sentence at the top of the paper along with a grade, with no other marks or comments. Most would include some comment to the student. Many would give two grades—content over conventions.

When I handed back the papers (after too long), the students, trained as they are in the ways of *school*, would feel that this grade summed up their work on this task and represented their achievement in this unit. I would feel virtuous, having spent so many hours correcting papers. Although I would have a good evaluation of each student's final paper, I would not feel that I had a clear sense of what students had learned or how effectively they had read.

A different model. What is happening in the classrooms of teachers who, uncomfortable with the previous model, are attempting to account for the activities of the whole task? Who believe that we must assess each student in terms of what that student brought to a particular assignment? Who see process as an important part of what we are about? Who know that reading and writing may be communally achieved? How might such a teacher approach the assessment of her students?

The keys to this kind of assessment are in having a clear set of performance standards to begin with, then in setting up a recording system that is not too cumbersome or time-consuming to be useful. (The California Learning Record task force, described in Chapter Seven, is well on its way toward developing such a record-keeping format. It has already been piloted and critiqued by teachers.) For the computer-adept, a file can be set up for each student. Teachers who use this system tell me that it works well for them to enter notes in student files throughout the day as they observe student engagement or confer with students. Other teachers prefer to keep a looseleaf notebook with file tabs for each student. The important thing is to get into the habit of making frequent, short, observational entries on the spot, using a preestablished list of performances. A suggested list of performances that both teachers and students may use as a check list appears at the end of this chapter. Not all of these performances, of course, will be observed in each phase of a complex assignment, but they are marks of the kinds of thinking that show productive engagement in literacy tasks. With this list, teachers can construct scales or rubrics to show levels of performance.

What might such a model look like when applied to the multifaceted task of reading "Bread"? As this second kind of teacher, I would give no grade to any of the component parts of this unit. I would, however, assemble a number of assessment notes throughout the project.

Responding to logs

- I would read and respond to some of the logs. I would not attempt to read all of the log entries for each student.
- Students would be in the habit of marking logs for me to respond to; I would read all logs students marked for my reading.
- I would read at least two or three of the seven logs for each student.

Team observations. I would be observant during the team sessions. I would be looking for the behaviors described at the end of the chapter in the teacher observation chart and in the "Literacy Performances." If I were a computer person, I would make quick entries for particular behaviors that I noticed during a class period. Otherwise, I would rely on notes made in my learning record for each student.

Graphics. Class presentations of graphics are critical. Here again, I would make notes, particularly when a student demonstrated a new insight or used metaphors in an unusual way. I would be looking for growth in metaphorical thinking and in the ability to translate graphics representing conceptual thinking into language.

Final projects. A final project is an opportunity for a student to integrate various aspects of a subject. I would evaluate it on the basis of how the form and content interrelate. I would look for risk-taking. I would be alert to growth spurts, or seeming setbacks, and would discuss those with the students. I would, again, use the Literacy Performances as a basis for evaluation.

Student reflection. The most important part of the evaluation would be the student's analysis of his or her own learning. (I suggest the student project evaluation form at the end of this chapter.) The student should be familiar with the criteria set forth at the beginning of the task. Given the realities of a high school teacher's class load, I would not plan to have a conference with each student at the end of each task. I would, however, have ample opportunities during the task to talk with each student several times. If the student's final evaluation of his or her learning seemed in any way off the mark to me, on the basis of my observations, I would set up a conference to discuss our divergent views.

Reality check: Assigning a grade. In a school where the teacher must assign quarter and semester grades (most high schools, at this time), I would take the responsibility for assigning a final grade for the project, using a holistic method of assessment based on a rubric built from the Literacy Performances and the teacher observation chart that appear at the end of this chapter. In contrast to the method of assigning a grade described earlier, which was largely (and probably fairly accurately) intuitive, this assessment would be based on criteria that the student and I had used together, that I could easily explain to an administrator or parent, and that could be applied fairly to all students engaged in the task. The student's self-evaluation, along with self-selected papers from the entire project, would go into the portfolio to become part of the data that would affect his or her final assessment for the course.

Structuring and Assessing
a Thematic Assignment:
The Icarus Project

The following assignment is based totally on the use of teams to accomplish its goals. This project design may be applied to any study
of a group of related works. In this case, the teacher provides the
specific works to be studied; in many situations, students would,
themselves, be responsible for collecting several works to illustrate
a myth or theme.

The assignment: Arrange the class in teams of four or five. Each
team will receive copies of the following seven poems as well as
Ovid's rendition of the myth of Icarus:

"The Story of Icarus," from the *Metamorphoses*	Ovid
"Landscape with the Fall of Icarus"	William Carlos Williams
"Lines on Breughel's 'Icarus'"	Michael Hamburger
"Musee des Beaux Arts"	W. H. Auden
"Icarus"	Lyman Andrews
"To a Friend Whose Work Has Come to Triumph"	Anne Sexton
"Icarus, come with me"	Bill Whiteman
"Icarus"	Edward Field

Directions for the team: Read at least four of the poems in the
Icarus collection. Each team member should take primary responsibility for one poem. Each member of the team should read his or her
poem aloud to the team. After listening to the poems, discuss them in
the team. Each participant should take responsibility for leading the
discussion of his or her selected poem. Then discuss the poems, using such questions as these: What do all the poems have in common? How do they differ? Talk briefly about these questions and
others that you pose for yourselves.

Each member of the team: Be the Icarus of your poem. Write a line
or two that Icarus might say. Specify the person Icarus might say this
line to. It could be anyone—Daedalus, the reader of the poem, his
mother (his mother? Icarus had a mother?), the Sun, and so on.
Share these lines with the team.

As a team: Read the assignment and decide how you can best accomplish it.

Team Assignment
Create a graphic that does the following things:

- shows the basic myth behind the poetic versions you have read
- depicts how each of the poets you selected viewed the story
- Includes the lines each member of the team wrote

Present your graphic to the rest of the class. Each member of the team should take some responsibility in the presentation.

Evaluation
Write an evaluation of this project to include in your portfolio. In this paper, use the following suggestions as a guide. Rather than respond to each of these suggestions separately, integrate them in your reflections about the project. Be sure to include anything else you think is important.

- Specify and comment on the poem that you selected.
- Explain the line that you wrote in the persona of Icarus.
- Evaluate your contribution to the graphic and to the presentation.
- Comment on the contributions made by other members of your team.
- Evaluate the graphic and presentation of your team.
- What did you learn from the other presentations?
- What did you learn from participating in this project?
- What questions did this project raise for you?

In my evaluation of individual student performance on the Icarus Project, I would rely on three things: my observations during the project, student reflections, and the team presentation. I would evaluate all students in each team on the graphic, using appropriate literacy performances from the list that appears at the end of this chapter.

Applying the Team Approach to the Study of a Novel

Integrating various individual and group strategies into a team approach to studying a novel creates a dynamic learning environment. On a personal note, I want to share my experience in teaching James Joyce's *A Portrait of the Artist as a Young Man*. For a number of years, I had "taught" *Portrait* to my Advanced Placement seniors. Although I used a number of graphic strategies and discussion groups, my focus was primarily on the writing of individual analytical papers of the sort that all of us wrote in college. As this novel is one of my favorites, I also lectured rather extensively, even though that was not my usual method of teaching; I thought that students needed the benefit of the critics' views, distilled through my own voice, for such a "difficult" novel. As I became more and more familiar with the constructivist approach to reading, I became increasingly uncomfortable lecturing on the novel. One year I decided to go cold turkey and implement a project approach to the novel that would be compatible with my beliefs about teaching reading. The results, as you might already have guessed, exceeded my expectations. Students were able not only to read, discuss, construct and explain graphics, but also to engage in criticism of the most penetrating nature. Their final papers far exceeded those of previous classes; they were rich with personal and literary connections, metaphoric thinking and a level of aesthetic appreciation that truly stunned me. My role was that of the expert contributor to group discussion, the poser of questions, the maker of suggestions for further exploration, but it was not that of interpreter. The students could do that themselves.

Here is an outline of the kinds of activities that I now use in teaching any novel. The outline is based on James Joyce's *Portrait of the Artist.*

Pre-reading: *Clustering* Possibilities
                  Cluster: the word *artist*
                  Cluster: the phrase *growing up*

Reading: Keep a Dialectical Journal as you read.
                  In your journal, trace one of the following as you read:
                        images of flight, color, art, sight, religion, politics

Discussion: Use your journals as a basis for your team discussions each day.

Re-reading: *Mapping* Possibilities: Individuals, partners, or teams
                  Map: the story line of the book
                  Map: the novel according to
                      1. the idea of "flight"
                      2. the author's use of color
                      3. the political aspects of the novel
                      4. the role of religion as it affects Stephen Daedalus
                  Map: the character of Stephen; include
                      1. his *actions*

2. his *thoughts* and *speech*
3. what *other characters* think about him
4. his *habits* or *behavior patterns*
5. *similes* or *metaphors* for the character (see sun-shadow mandala)
6. the relationship of Stephen to the myth of Daedalus and Icarus

Note: Use quotations from the book on your map; give page references.

Modeling for Understanding Style:

Emulation: Select passage that is characteristic of the author's style. Model a passage word for word, using a completely different subject. Following the emulation, continue the modeled passage, attempting to retain the stylistic tone of the original.

Character Study Mandala

Create a sun-shadow mandala for Stephen (see Appendix One).

Suggestions for Team Study

Reading/Interpretation Teams

After students have completed a first reading of the entire book, assign each team one chapter of the book. The teams will be responsible for these activities:

1. Giving their section of the book a title. This activity requires close rereading to decide on the primary importance of that chapter.
2. Creating a graphic for the chapter. This activity requires discussion to determine primary *events, character interactions, dominant symbols, significant quotations,* and so on. Graphics must convey the essence of the assigned chapter of the book as well as specific information about it.
3. Presenting the team graphic to the rest of the class. This step is a vital one for the presenting team as well as for the other teams; insights often emerge from this stage of the study as the students stand back and interpret their own work. As each team presents, they involve the entire class in discussion, moving back and forward in the book as events affect the chapter they are presenting.

4. Creating and presenting a dramatic, poetic, or musical experience to convey the team members' understanding and internalization of some aspect their study, not limited now to their particular chapter. (This section may be held as the last activity,
following the individual writing of papers.)

Examples of team presentations from the study of *Portrait:*

- a graphic portrayal of the continuing Catholic/Protestant conflict in Ireland
- a reading of original poems stemming from ideas generated by
the study of the novel
- a dramatic presentation of the myth of Daedalus and Icarus, showing how Joyce has integrated aspects of both Daedalus and Icarus
into the character of Stephen

Writing Teams

After the graphic and dramatic presentations, teams are disbanded
and re-formed, jigsaw fashion, each new team to contain one member
of each old team. This structure ensures that the new "writing teams"
will have expert representatives from all sections of the novel. The
team brainstorms ideas for writing related to the study of the entire
novel. Each student is responsible for a major writing assignment,
but the team will serve as support system at all stages of the generation of the work. Students may elect to write one major paper or
prepare a portfolio of smaller works, perhaps a combination of essays and poems. Students are encouraged to select their areas of interest, then decide which form would be most effective. Their
audience is other members of the class as well as another class with
which they frequently interact, exchanging written as well as oral
presentations. Here are some examples of papers that students have
written in response to *Portrait;* I have formulated their positions as
writing prompts.

Interpretation

Write a formal paper analyzing some aspect of the novel that in-
trigues you. Use your dialectical journal as well as your map for
ideas. In this paper, follow the rules for a conventional paper, using
the text for support of your ideas; be sure to follow established
guidelines for quotations, references, and so forth.

Autobiographical Incident

1. Select a scene from the novel showing Stephen as a young boy and write a personal account of a parallel experience in your own life.
2. Select a myth with which you identify; write an autobiographical incident that shows the parallel between your own experience and the myth.

Poetry

1. Weave the sun and shadow mandala images of Stephen into a poem.
2. Write a series of haiku or diamond poems for Stephen using the sun-shadow images. For example, the animal haiku should embody both the sun and shadow images of animals. (See sun-shadow mandala instructions in Appendix One.)
3. Write a poetic dialogue between the inner and outer aspects of Stephen (the sun and the shadow); or write a poetic dialogue between yourself and Stephen, using a running outer (aloud) and inner (thoughts only) speech. (Based on the sun-shadow mandala.)
4. Look back over your dialectical journal and find responses that you might use in writing a poem or series of poems.

Speculation about Effects

Write a paper speculating on Stephen's life ten years (or some other number of years) into the future. Ground your speculations in actual events in the novel.

Narrative Speculation

Write a Chapter 6, based on your speculations about Stephen's future.

Literacy Performances for an Integrated Task

Be mindful observers as you look for these behaviors, marks of engaging in a transactive way with the work of the project. To what degree does the student:

1. Engage in all four functions: observe, analyze, imagine, and feel.

2. Demonstrate engagement with the task by experimenting with ideas: think divergently; take risks; express opinions (e.g., speculate, hypothesize, explore alternative scenarios; raise questions; make predictions; think metaphorically).

3. Explore ambiguities and multiple possibilities of meaning; consider cultural and/or psychological nuances and complexities in the task.

4. Make connections between the task and previously held ideas, knowledge, and personal experiences.

5. Clarify purpose; revise, reshape, and/or deepen early understanding of the task.

6. Challenge the task by agreeing or disagreeing, arguing, endorsing, questioning, and wondering.

7. Demonstrate understanding of the task as a whole.

8. Show aesthetic appreciation of texts or other works being studied; consider linguistic and structural complexities.

9. Use the appropriate rhetorical stance in speaking and writing; fulfill the rhetorical requirements of the task.

10. Reflect on the meaning(s) of the task, including a possible universal significance; express a major understanding or insight.

Teacher Observation Chart for Team Projects

Observation Category	Student	Student	Student	Student	Student
Assumes leadership role					
Demonstrates effective leadership style (specify)					
Contributes ideas					
Contributes work such as drawing, filming					
Contributes to the class presentation					
Demonstrates comprehension					
Demonstrates grasp of details					
Demonstrates facility in working as team member					
Demonstrates particular talent (specify)					
Demonstrates ability to articulate ideas					
Demonstrates ability to synthesize ideas					

STUDENT PROJECT EVALUATION

Name _____ Period _____ Date _____

Project Title: _____

List members of team and indicate their degree of participation in the project as well as their contributions in terms of leadership, willingness to work, creativity, or other special area (such as expertise in filming). Rank contributions in range of 5 (high) to 1 (low).

Team Members	Degree of Participation	Leadership	Willingness to Work	Creativity	Other Contributions (Specify)
Self					

On a separate page, describe the process that your team went through in completing this project. Include how you made your decisions about the subject of your project, research needed, talents needed to carry out your ideas, and anything else that affected the way you worked. What did you do when things didn't turn out as expected, for instance? The focus here is on how you worked together as a team. Be sure to include your part in the process.

STUDENT PROJECT EVALUATION, PAGE 2

Name _____ Period _____ Date _____

Project Title: _____

Evaluate your project in terms of the following: (5=high; 1=low). In the column at the right, explain your evaluation.

Project Qualities	Evaluation	Explanation
Information presented		
Creativity in presentation		
Overall effectiveness of presentation (written)		
Overall effectiveness of presentation (visual)		
Overall effectiveness of presentation (oral)		

Explain what you learned as a result of doing this project.

Chapter Five

Classroom Portfolios
From Self-Discovery
to Self-Assessment

This chapter presents one teacher's approach to the use of classroom portfolios. Joan Brown, teacher at Alameda High School in Alameda, California, has worked extensively with the classroom portfolio as a way of helping students become aware of and take responsibility for their own learning. In this chapter she provides us with a distillation of her experience with the portfolio as an integral part of the assessment process.

Joan Brown

PORTFOLIO: a collection of works deliberately selected and arranged for a particular purpose, for use by and identified reader or readers. The compiler often includes some explanatory or reflective material to set a context for the portfolio and/or for the individual pieces it contains.

Perhaps more than any other activity, portfolios allow for and reward the diversity that we find in our classrooms. Portfolios, with their breadth of presentation methods, allow us as teachers to validate all kinds of learning, all kinds of expression. They encourage varying modes of expression—the written, the oral, the graphic, the three-dimensional model, the video, the audio. They allow students with differing learning styles to show that they've learned and how they've learned it. They also allow students to validate their own primary way of knowing, and to gain expanded awareness and understanding of other ways of knowing. In addition, portfolios allow language-reluctant students to show what they know through diagrams, graphics, models, and maps; they also allow "discipline-reluctant" students (e.g., the "mathophobic") to use words to show their grasp of mechanical concepts, even if they haven't yet mastered the manipulation of the figures.

It is imperative that we build into our classrooms time to reflect. We must give students time to think about and respond to the way they work and what they produce if they are to have a valid and ongoing awareness and record of their own learning. Portfolios can serve as tools through which the author and the reader can examine curriculum and learning, effort and improvement, process and product. They are vehicles of ongoing assessment, engaging students in activities of observing and selecting, interpreting and comparing, reflecting and evaluating. They promote student ownership of learning, and they allow for diversity in requiring the student to choose works to be included; they provide an anchor in encouraging both teachers and students to examine the curriculum as they establish a purpose for the classroom portfolio.

The portfolio begins with the folder, the storehouse in which students save all of their work. Drafts of assignments, scribblings, reading responses, journal entries, final papers, graphics, exams, and ongoing responses to assignments all are saved in a folder. In addition, in preparation for looking at their entire growth as learners, students may save and respond to pivotal assignments from classes other than English.

The actual process of compiling and shaping the portfolio is a culminating activity, focused and finalized at the end of a term; however, like the assignments that appear in the portfolio, the reflection and self-assessment are an integral part of day-to-day classroom activities. I ask students to annotate their major assignments before they turn them in, noting questions and comments and places where they want specific response from me. I also ask them to respond metacognitively to the assignment itself—noting the way they worked as they proceeded through it, and recording their thoughts about their final product. These notes, captured as the students are engaged in the process, are invaluable benchmarks when students later return to the assignment and re-vision their responses to it from a distance of time.

Students keep a metacognitive log throughout the year in which they examine, explore, and assess their own processes of responding and learning in my classroom, in other classes, and in their worlds outside of school. At the end of a term, when students turn to their folders to begin to shape their portfolios, these log entries provide a history of the student's responses to learning. They can be the genesis for both the students' choices of assignments to include and for their reflection that will shape the final portfolio. In addition, such logs give students an alternative to simply quitting when they are stumped on an assignment. They can turn to their logs and write about "what I do when I can't do what I'm supposed to do" or free-write about their frustrations and questions about the assignment; they can submit this entry to me in place of the aborted homework assignment. Often students discover the generative properties of writing, spontaneously answering their own questions in their journals; always such entries are an indication that students are actively involved in their own processes as they grapple with the tasks facing them.

When the time is right, usually at the end of a unit or a term, we set a purpose for the portfolio and students go through their folders, their annotations, and their logs to select, organize, and respond to the pieces they choose to include. If a parent, peer, or other outside response is to be part of the portfolio, students determine the kind of information they want from these people, contact them, and include these responses in the portfolio along with their own reflections and assessment of the processes. When students bring their finished portfolios to class, they revel in their accomplishments as they share and respond to each others' work, again revisiting their own learning experiences through sharing the learning experiences of others.

The shapes, the sizes, the styles of portfolios are as varied as the content material of our classrooms. Portfolio pieces can be arranged chronologically or thematically; they can move from the simple to the complex, or from the drafts of pieces to the polished products; they might be organized according to subject matter or to genre of writing, or according to the specific kinds of activities the particular pieces represent. The possibilities are vast, governed by the purpose established by the student and the teacher, guided by the picture that the student chooses to put forward of his or her work over a given period, and limited only by the imaginations of the portfolio creators.

Purpose Governs Product: Kinds of Portfolios

There are, essentially, two kinds of individual classroom portfolios; however, there are many variations on each of these themes. In showcase portfolios, authors select their best examples of particular kinds of work. In formative or growth portfolios, authors show development in a particular tangible area or areas over a specific period. In the world of business, the showcase portfolio is what one presents to a prospective employer to get the job. The formative portfolio is what one presents to a supervisor to show progress in a given job-related area, perhaps in response to a comment on an employee review sheet, or to convince a superior to grant a merit raise

Within these two broad types of classroom portfolios lies a wide range of possibilities, depending of the breadth of focus that the author wants. Each of these portfolio types can be designed with a single focus, to show the process of growth in a single area or mastery of a particular kind (e. g., interpretive writing, pencil drawing, lab analysis); or they can have multiple purposes and be organized to show growth in a variety of areas or to showcase a variety of elements mastered in that period. The possibilities are broad, governed by the purpose chosen by the student and the teacher, and guided by the self-portrait that the student chooses to put forward through the presentation of this particular portfolio.

The Showcase Portfolio

In a *showcase portfolio*, the author strives to show mastery of things taught and learned during a given period. Such a portfolio, a compilation of work successfully completed, is a valuable tool in applying for a job or in applying to college. Unlike the formative portfolio, the showcase features only the author's best works— works that show the pinnacle of achievement in predetermined areas. For instance, such a portfolio might show a student's mastery of writing, including papers representing a broad range of writing types, from a broad range of disciplines, each a sample of excellence in its area. Or such a portfolio might show a student's mastery of Earth Science, presenting a compilation of the best examples of the student's work done in that class during the given period. In either case, the portfolio is a showcase, with assignments representing the best work available and with reflections that focus on the importance of the feature that was mastered, while still including some discussion of the process that went into its mastery.

The Formative Portfolio

The process portfolio, unlike the showcase portfolio, shows the author's process of working in a given area over time, along with all of the deadends, frustrations, and moments of satisfaction, pride, and relief that come with achieving growth. The area(s) of growth to be examined can be determined by the teacher and/or by the student, emerging from the curriculum content and from student-determined learning goals. For example, one type of formative portfolio might show a student's growth as an English student, drawing on assignments ranging from reading and writing responses to graphic activities or essays of different types. Another might have a specific curricular focus, showing a student's growth as a writer, or, even more specifically, as a writer of interpretation. In math such a portfolio might track a student's growing understanding of proofs in geometry; in science it might show the student's developing grasp of the physics of bridges. Such portfolios might track a single class project from beginning to end, including the requisite personal reflection, or they might present a sequence of activities deliberately chosen to show the ups and downs of the student's developing understanding. Once the focus of the portfolio is established, students choose and arrange work to reflect their growth and change in that area or areas.

And Yet Another Possibility for the Classroom: The Class Portfolio

The *class portfolio* is an activity that allows students to work together as a class to revisit, examine, and evaluate the activities and learning processes of a given period, exploring the growth and achievement of the classroom group as a whole. At the end of class projects, the class itself can pull together a portfolio in which students and the teacher work together to gather materials that represent the experience of the entire class. Like other portfolios, the class portfolio might be a formative portfolio, focusing on one element of the classroom experience (e. g., writing, problem solving, etc.), or it can reflect the breadth of classroom experience during that period, featuring examples of each type of work produced during the unit (e. g., group work, journal writings, lab notes, final papers, etc.). The class portfolio might also be a showcase portfolio containing the best work by each student during the period; or it might be a combination of these two. Because this is a class effort, it is imperative that each student be represented in the final portfolio. Whenever possible, I reproduce these for students, who generally want to have a copy, and sometimes we "publish" them on the walls of the classroom or give a copy to the Media Center as examples of student work.

So How Do We Grade Them?
The Teacher-Assessment Component

Portfolios by their nature allow for diversity in every area of their production and their assessment. They provide us with a situation in which there need be no competition, no "curving" of the grade or external standards against which the student need be measured. Student reflection and self-assessment is threaded throughout the portfolio, and each individual's portfolio is measured against the purpose that the student set for him- or herself in that particular portfolio. I assess classroom portfolios holistically, although they might also be assessed analytically, on a rating scale designed for a specific portfolio assignment. In either case, there must always be honest teacher response both to individual items in the portfolio and to the portfolio as a whole. Most of the time I respond on Post-its™ notes to honor the care students take in the presentation of their materials.

If you are grading holistically, it's a good idea to develop a rubric with students as they are engaged in the portfolio process. This procedure can help refocus students on the requirements for the portfolio they're preparing, and it gives them ownership of the assessment process. You might consider the following in developing a scoring rubric:

- Is everything there?
- Are the reflections and self-assessment sincere, insightful, and real?
- Is the portfolio organized with a clear purpose?
- Do the selected items, taken as a whole, accomplish the stated purpose?
- Is the presentation attractive?
- Do the selected items reflect a breadth of activity and learning?
- Does the portfolio demonstrate an awareness of audience?
- Does the portfolio display the author's attention to details and care in communicating?

From answers to such questions, the teacher and the class can work together to develop a rubric. (Six-point scales work well with students; they have been used by many teachers who have scored large-scale assessments with 6-point scales.)

It is important to note that my assessment of a student's portfolio is not an assessment of the individual assignments that the student has included in the portfolio. I have already evaluated these throughout the course of the term as the assignments were made.

Rather, in reading a classroom portfolio, I am assessing the degree to which the student accomplishes his or her stated purpose in presenting the portfolio to me. I try to allow the students to speak to me through their work, introducing themselves and their purpose through the preface, showing a breadth of growth and activity through the choices of entries and the reflections about those entries, and reflecting on the process as a whole revealed in the self-assessment threaded throughout and in the end-letter. I respond to the breadth and appropriateness of selections the student has made, to the honesty of reflection, to the cohesiveness of the whole in presenting the intended picture of the student's learning.

I do not correct portfolios, nor do I change them in any way. Rather, I respond to them, commenting on student ideas, questioning things I don't understand, and sharing my own ideas and responses to their ideas as these occur to me. For me these are soft (though not "easy") evaluations. I read student portfolios slowly; I enjoy them. The evaluations emerge easily, intuitively, fairly, as honest responses to students' presentations of themselves.

What to Put in There: The Common Elements of Portfolios

A portfolio is a collection of works deliberately selected for a particular purpose and arranged according to a recognizable plan, for use by an identified reader or readers. Whereas the folder is a storehouse of materials, the portfolio is a compilation of works selected in order to impart a particular impression of the creator to a specific audience. Its structure, its contents, and its organizational pattern are all deliberately chosen to accomplish a specific end.

Although the shapes, the sizes, and the styles of portfolios are as varied as the content material of our classrooms, most portfolios, regardless of the purpose, should contain the following six elements:

- a preface through which the student focuses the purpose of this particular portfolio, tells the story of creating the portfolio, and reflects on both the processes and product represented by the portfolio
- a table of contents
- selections of work
- reflection, often included with each individual selection, exploring the impact and relevance of that particular selection to this particular portfolio

- self-assessment
- an end-letter

The Preface

The *preface* is an informal but major work of synthesis and sub-
stance, through which students introduce themselves and their
portfolios, tell the story of their process of compiling the portfolio,
and include a measure of self-assessment in which they evaluate
their participation and growth during the period represented in this
particular portfolio. In this entry, students explain the focus and the
purpose of this particular portfolio, clarifying for the audience why
they have done what they have done and explaining the way in
which they have chosen to exhibit their work. Although the preface
is the first major entry in the portfolio, it is the last piece that students compose, for it is through the composition of this piece that
students take a final, somewhat distanced and objective look at the
picture of themselves they have presented through the portfolio
they have created.

Although some self-assessment is threaded throughout the portfolio, the self-assessment component of the preface is pivotal, as it
enables students to revisit and evaluate the "whole" of their experience after having revisited individual pieces of their experience as
a part of compiling the portfolio. I do not often ask students to assign themselves a grade for the portfolio, although I do make it clear
to them that their portfolio grade can certainly be a negotiated set-
tlement. Having them focus on "grading" themselves rather than
"assessing" themselves diverts them somewhat from the reflective,
exploratory nature of true self-assessment. It moves students in the
direction of justifying the grade that they choose. In explaining the
self-assessment component of the preface to students, I might say

> Now that you've compiled your portfolio and are reviewing your
> body of work, preparatory to writing your preface, evaluate your
> tenure in this class during this period. As you revisit the things
> we've done, consider your interest in them, the value they have in
> your life in this classroom, in other classes, and in other areas of
> your life. Consider the degree of your participation and the qual-
> ity of your performance, your consistency and dependability as
> represented by the pieces here included. What risks have you
> taken? What have you put in? What have you taken out? To what
> extent do the pieces you've included here show you voicing your
> own ideas and shaping your own education? How are you differ-
> ent now from the way you were when you began the work repre-

sented in this portfolio? You might refer specifically to papers and projects included in your portfolio, elaborating on your reflections and/or assessments of a paper/project's interest or value. You might comment on reasons for your involvement or lack of involvement, perhaps, explaining why you have assessed the quality of your work as you have.

Here are two prefaces, both clearly from students who have valued the process.

Portfolio Preface

by Yvonne Tsang, Grade 10

I can't believe my year in English 2EXP is over. The 9000 minutes are almost up, but I've spent many more minutes doing work related to this class outside of the room . . . and I will probably continue to.

The way this class was run surprised me at first. We had to be more independent and we had to take charge of our own education. I didn't realize that in the beginning, but now I do. And that applies to many classes, not just this one.

Some of the assignments and projects we did will always stand out in my memory, like the project on my mother and the one on Asher Lev. They will stand out because they have a deep meaning to me; I really cared about those projects. I put a lot of time into them, and I *learned.* I could almost *feel* myself grow.

I have grown a lot this year, in many ways. This class was part of my growth. I think differently—more critically, more questioningly, and I make connections without thinking about it. Sometimes I connect part of a movie to something I read in class. I connect concepts from *The Odyssey* to my own life. At first it was kind of creepy. I surprised myself with my thoughts; all of a sudden I would think, "I'm trapped within two places . . like Scylla and Charybdis." And then I connected concepts we discussed like inner peace, the hero, the journey (Ithaca), etc. I was surprised I remembered them, and now I seem to see them everywhere.

I'm still a quiet person in classes. I don't know when or if that will change. But towards the end of the year I did start to speak up a little, and at times voluntarily, not even thinking about points or grades. Everyone was surprised when you began oral participation points, but it did make our class more lively. I do wish we had risked talking more with each other—everyone in our class is so talented, and now I realize we could have learned a lot from each other—but to take the risk of publicly being "wrong"—well, I guess that was particularly hard for this intensely competitive group of people. But I know that was our choice. We took hold of our education and we chose to be independent learners and thinkers. I suppose that isn't always bad, but it just hit me—that's what bigotry and racism are made from—ignorance of others and refusal to be open-minded and learn from others. That *just* hit me. It's scary. I don't think we'll grow up to be bigots and racists of course, but. . . we might be closed minded if we lock ourselves and our talents up. These are scary thoughts. I really do think too much that I scare myself sometimes.

Anyway, I guess I haven't taken many risks either. It's just the way I am. Looking back, however, I see that all I risked was a better education.

Last year I interviewed Mrs. Tillotson for *The Oak Leaf* (it was a story on retiring teachers) and she also said something I will not forget: "You get out of any class what you put into it." I think I have put a lot into this class—for myself. But I got a lot out of it also. I am starting to feel guilty that I was being selfish for not speaking up and sharing. I learned a lot, but it was mostly from myself and you. That isn't bad, but we also could have taught each other a lot. But it's too late now—at least for this year.

This class was an incredible experience. I really don't like assigning myself grades. I expect to get A's and I work hard for them, but I don't like to sound conceited by giving myself A's, and I don't want to give myself less than I deserved. I came into this class thinking, hoping, that I'd get an A and knowing that I'd do all the required work to get an A. What I hadn't expected was to have to risk discovering "hows" and "whys" for myself as well as producing assigned "whats." Regardless of the grade (and I guess I'd give myself an A), this class is Ithaca, and Constantine Cavafy was right—the journey is more important than the pre-set goal or arrival.

Portfolio Preface

by Lun Chuang, Grade 10

The boy stepped into a room of strangers. Fourteen pairs of eyes glued themselves to his form. They notice his too-large bag slung over his shoulders, his neat attire, his wire-frame glasses, and the piece of paper clutched uncertainly in his left hand. He was a stranger to them as well. Then the teacher took charge. It was September 5th .

And now it is June 9th. A whole school year has flashed by in what seems like a matter of minutes. And in this school year much has happened, some good, some bad. There was a decision I made early in the year that now I find no cause to regret—my decision to enter Honors English.

I have always had a love for the English language, and the EXP class seemed a great place to be. And I have enjoyed every day of it since. There are memories from this course, this classroom that I will carry with me far into the future. There are friendships made in here that I will treasure for life. There is a great teacher that I will always remember.

From the beginning I have worked hard in this class to produce quality work each time I produce any work. I try to put the utmost of everything I have into whatever I do—whether it is a poem, an interpretive essay, a sketch, a mandala, or any of the other engaging, engrossing things we've done in this class. I go for 100%—it is in my blood; without doing so, I would not gain peace in my heart. The satisfaction I crave can only be earned through hard work and determination. As the work piled on, so did the time I spent pile on proportionally. At times the pressures were tremendous and the thought of giving up was strong. But always when I attained my ends, I also obtained a bliss of unimaginable sweetness, well worth the effort I had spent.

Hard work has always been *in* me. But one thing I learned from this class which I believe is important is the value of eager participation. My teacher always had trouble getting students in the class to speak out, to take the risks, to venture out of our shells. I was part of the silence as well, unable to break free, reluctant to break free. Her efforts to push us into the open succeeded in the end, and I began to speak and share more. I began to feel the effects of speaking out. No more lingering, unanswered questions. No more uncertainty. Gone also were the patches of silence that hung over us since day one. This was, to me, the greatest lesson of this year for me—to risk speaking out. It has so many positive attributes to offer, and none of the negative ones.

When I step out of this class, the things I learned from it will remain for a long time. This class prompted and lured my creativity out. It made me think about myself, about others around me, about the world. It taught me the many different ways to see an object or a piece of literature, and it made me see the many ways people can view my own work. It taught me how to present my opinions and ideas in a clear and concise manner. I am grateful to a special teacher.

If someone asked me about this class, I would say one thing to them, one thing more than enough to convey the greatness of it all: A+!
Thank you, Mrs. Brown!

Table of Contents

Students determine the organization of the portfolio; however, both the table of contents and the organization of materials must be purposeful. Because the portfolio is meant to highlight certain areas, I limit the number of entries students can include, usually to nine or ten "tangibles" and three or four "intangibles." In addition to keeping the portfolios to a manageable length, this limitation encourages students to choose their selections deliberately and purposefully.

Selections of Work

The tangibles. The *tangibles* are the specific written assignments or other tangible examples of activities that the student has chosen to include in the portfolio. Students draw these from their folders, according to the purpose and direction they've established for their portfolio. In most instances I have previously responded to and graded these artifacts, and students do not revise them to include them in the portfolio. They are inserted "as is," that is, with all of the notations, grades, and comments written on them. Such tangible entries might include graded written assignments, exams, graphics, and/or projects (or photographs of graphics or projects that cannot be included because of their size). Sometimes I allow students free reign in choosing a given number of tangibles to include; other times I require that certain assignments or examples of assignments be included, leaving some openings or "wild cards" for their choice. As always, the purpose of the portfolio determines the choices of tangible assignments that the student will include.

Some possibilities:

- A piece from which you learned something about your own *process* of learning
- A piece that involved you in problem solving individually or as a member of a group
- A piece that represents your "typical" work during this period (or during each quarter)
- A piece that represents your best writing, lab work, and so forth.
- Two pieces that, taken together, show your growth as a writer (scientist, mathematician, etc.). Compare these two pieces, examining both the similarities and the differences, the strengths and the weaknesses. Then, write a brief reflection in which you consider the reasons for the change and the direction in which you want to move in the future.

- Your favorite piece of work
- A piece that represents a particularly creative process or product growing from this class—a graphic, a model, a video, and so on.
- A piece that reflects your participation in a group project
- A full-process piece, with all of the steps, dead ends, and all
- A piece that reflects something you did or learned in English class that is also valuable to you in another discipline
- A piece from another discipline that is appropriate to this classroom as well. This piece might range from a note-taking technique or a graphic to a reflection on a piece of scientific writing, to an examination of a scientist's process of discovery as you examine a character in literature. Tune into analytic processes that you use outside of this classroom—and even outside of this school in your "other" life. Let your reflection on this piece reflect both what you learned from doing the piece originally, and how that knowledge is related to this class.

These tangible examples of work form the foundation of the portfolio. They can range from final copies of written work to notes or cards that represent breakthroughs in thinking, to snapshots or descriptions of graphics or projects that are too large to include in the portfolio. Whatever their size or their form, these pieces are chosen with purpose and with care to develop the picture of the student that he or she has established in the preface of the portfolio. Students accompany each piece with a reflective response through which they explore the importance of the piece to this particular portfolio. Through such commentary students reflect on their feelings about the work as they look back on it, as well as reflecting on how they created it.

The intangible moments. "School," a student of mine once commented, "is the five minutes between classes, lunch, and brunch. Classes are just the things we have to sit through in order to get to the real world of the hallways, the cafeteria, and our lockers." There is a great deal of truth to this student's comment; in fact, a great deal of a student's growth and learning takes place quietly, internally, never to be captured in a tangible paper or product. It is important that students recognize that school is far more than the sum of the products that they produce, that their learning is represented by experiences that often are not captured in a tangible product. To this end, in addition to the tangible products that students include in their portfolios, I ask students to include accounts of several *intangible moments* that were pivotal in their growth or mastery during the portfolio period. These might be moments in the classroom, or outside of the classroom when students have been focused on the classroom. They are moments that mattered to the student, moments that will continue to impact them in their approaches to learning, to their education, to their thinking, their reading, their writing, their lives.

Students write up these intangible moments as vignettes, no longer than one page each, focusing on recreating the moment of impact vividly so that the reader of the portfolio will "be" there to experience it. Students then follow the vignette with reflective commentary to clarify the impact and importance of the experience to the reader. Capturing such epiphanies, reexperiencing them and reflecting on their importance, can be invaluable in helping students broaden their own views of their educations and in sensitizing them to the kinds of learning that take place all of the time, both in and outside of the classroom.

Reflective Commentary

The reflection, which is threaded through every portion of the portfolio, is actually the most important part of both the portfolio process and product. It is this reflective commentary that most truly gives the portfolio audience a window to the "other side of the desk." It is through this commentary that students establish and maintain the focus of their portfolios, exploring and explaining how each of their selected pieces adds to the picture they are building of their own learning and mastery. The process of developing the reflective commentary is an invaluable learning experience for students: As they revisit a body of work, reexamine it with the added perspective of time, and explore its relevance, students gain both the time and the means of actually seeing their learning processes in action.

Reflection is an ongoing process in our classrooms. It comes in the form of journal entries and notes, self-assessments and logs, notes, memos, and annotations. On occasion I ask students to respond to specific parts of activities (e.g., experimental design portion of the problem-solving investigation; the revision part of the writing assignment). These mini-reflections are informal and quick, and they are kept, along with all student work, in their folders. Later, when students begin to gather materials for their portfolios, they revisit and perhaps revise these initial assessments in light of later activities.

I often use the headings of the self-assessment chart found in Appendix Six to allow students to capture their reflections of the moment; they look at their level of interest in the assignment, the level of value to them, the degree of their participation, and the quality of their participation. They generally chart all of their activities—papers, projects, graphics, presentations—before they begin the process of deciding which works to include in their portfolios. Sometimes I list the activities students are to chart; sometimes they do; sometimes we do it together. Completing this chart helps them focus on the reasons for their choices of entries and also provides thoughtful points for their reflections.

The portfolio assignment allows students time to revisit these initial reflections, whether they are charts or notes, annotations or log entries, to revise them with the benefit of distance as they focus their attention specifically on ways this particular experience might have affected their learning. As students develop and formalize these initial reflective responses, they focus their reflection to clarify how and why the piece now, long after its initial creation, belongs in this particular portfolio. Such a reflective process allows students to see how much more than a simple product a given assignment can be. They begin to understand the recursive, fluid quality of learning as they see how the cumulative effect of first creating the assignment and then deliberately selecting it for a particular purpose in the portfolio combine to reveal the breadth of its effect on their learning.

Self-Assessment throughout the Portfolio

Like reflection, self-assessment is an ongoing process in the classroom; and like reflection, self-assessment is generally threaded throughout the portfolio. Most portfolios include a statement of self-assessment in the preface, through which students evaluate their learning. On occasion I ask students to respond to directed questions to prompt their thinking about self-assessment. This process can be helpful for them in choosing the pieces they want to include in the portfolio as well as in focusing the self-assessment component of their preface. Other times I simply ask students to thread self-assessment through each part of their portfolio, exploring the degree of their participation and the quality of their performance as represented by the pieces included in the portfolio.

Whatever the technique, self-assessment is as integral a part of the portfolio process as reflection; and it is invaluable for students to engage in both self-assessment and reflection of the separate pieces as a way of arriving at a valid and honest self-assessment of the whole of their progress during a given period. The portfolio assignment provides students with an invaluable opportunity to step back and take a global view of their work with a specific eye toward as-sessing their participation, their growth, and their mastery. It allows them to see where they've been so they can better determine where they want to go.

Directed questions for self-assessment: Some possibilities.

- Describe how working with others improved your ability to un-derstand the concepts presented here.
- Describe how the processes and products in your portfolio reflect "real world" situations you have encountered or may encounter.
- Describe how this collection of documents shows your growth or mastery in a particular area (determined by the focus of the portfolio).
- What does this collection of documents tell you about where you want to go in your further study?
- In what ways has the preparation of your portfolio been a learn-ing and growth experience in itself?
- How would you change, improve, and/or adapt this portfolio project for next year's students?

The End-Letter and the Outside Input: "My Growth as a Learner"

In the end-letter to the portfolio, students step outside of the imme-diate purpose of their portfolios to examine their overall develop-ment as students. Drawing on different kinds of work from a variety of disciplines and integrating it with the work they've chosen for this particular portfolio, students explore their growing understanding of themselves in their broad role as students. They present this summa-ry reflection in the form of a letter written to a parent or a significant adult who stands outside of the school setting. The addressee is asked to respond as they would to any personal letter they received.

A sample end-letter assignment

Instructions to Students:
Your task is to write a letter to your parent(s) or to another significant non-school person in your life in which you share your impressions, reflections, and evaluations of your process and your progress during this semester. As you review your experiences during this semester to analyze and reflect on your growth as a student and as a whole person, you will of course draw on experiences you've had in En-glish; however, you may also draw on experiences you've had in

other subjects as well.

You might consider the following areas in which you may have grown and/or changed: you may have changed as

- a reader
- a writer
- a problem-solver
- a risk taker
- a class-builder
- a questioner
- a creator
- a creative thinker
- an independent learner
- an analytic thinker
- a collaborator
- a (think of your own word!)

Certainly you've experienced changes in all of these areas through this semester; however, as is the case with any paper, you'll need to find a focus—to discriminate and evaluate the most profound areas of impact to explore fully in your first-semester letter. So . . . choose two or three of these areas, or others—areas in which you see the most profound changes in your attitudes, processes, and products—and explore them in depth, reflecting on how you've changed and mentioning several specific assignments or intangible moments that have been pivotal for you in affecting your changes.

A word about tone and organization: You are writing a letter, so the tone will be conversational and informal. The focus is on you— you are sharing reflections about yourself—so you will use the vertical pronoun I as you explore ways in which you've changed and examine the experiences that have been catalysts for that change. Your letter, however, is not to be mere generalities or philosophical ramblings about your growth. As with any piece of writing, it must be organized around ideas, and those ideas must be explained with the use of specific examples.

You must, in other words, establish the focus of your letter in its opening paragraph. You must then anchor each section of your letter in one of the areas of growth you determine to examine; and you must fully validate your reflections by mentioning at least two or three specific assignments, projects, or moments to show how your growth in this area has come about and why this area seems particularly important to you at this time. Each assignment or experience that you mention must be placed in context. (Remember, your parents/friends don't know what class you're talking about or what the assignment was, so you need to tell them.) You must explicitly state the function of the experience—that is, how it contributed to your growth and/or change in the area you're discussing in that section of your paper—and you must explain reflectively why that particular experience had such an impact and was so pivotal as to merit mention in this letter.

For each of the areas you choose to address, mention at least two or three specific assignments from various disciplines that were pivotal; and include mention of at least one intangible moment that affected you in that way. You must have at least four or five assignments and at least two intangible moments detailed in your letter.

Throughout your letter, weave in reflections about the assignments and experiences you're sharing. What were the frustrations? The surprises? The successes? The failures? You are exploring the impact of these experiences on you as well as examining and interpreting how they've affected your growth in a particular area(s).

Finally, toward the ending of your letter, evaluate yourself as a participant in this semester's activities in your student life. This does not mean "give yourself a grade." Rather, it means make some generalizations about where you've been and where you are now, and set some goals for how you want to direct your energies during the next semester.

Please make two copies of your letter: one to give to me and one to share with your parent(s) or other significant adult. When you turn in your letter, please accompany it with the response written by the addressee of the letter.

A sample request to parents or primary care-givers

January 2, 1995
Dear Parents or Care-Givers:

As one portion of their final exam for this semester, I have asked students to write a letter sharing their impressions, reflections, and evaluations of their processes and their progress during this first semester of the 1994–95 school year. I've asked them to draw on experiences they've had in English and in other subjects as they review their experiences during the semester to analyze and reflect on their growth as a student.

Please take a few minutes to read and respond to this letter. Please make positive comments only; students get plenty of constructive criticism in the classroom. Your note need not be lengthy, but I hope that it will be responsive to the pride, frustrations, and reflections that reveal the student's ideas and feelings about what he or she has learned this term.

If you have questions or comments about this process, don't hesitate to contact me at home by telephone before 9:00 P.M. You have my number!

Portfolio End-Letter to Parent and Parent Response

by Angela Pryor-Nelson, Grade 10

Dear Mother,

During the first semester of the 1994–95 school year, my success and involvement at school have changed greatly. I have developed in many areas, including better organization of individual assignments and my schoolwork in general. Another area in which I have changed is group leadership. In many of the groups I have worked with, I am the only one with the desire for such skills and I am learning to use them.

Some of the assignments which have helped me with organizing my writing include the responses to *My Antonia* in my English class. In those responses I was to write about and give opinions as well as make reflections and assertions on what the book meant to me. As part of the process I had to annotate my own writing which gave me a clear idea of what I'd done and what I still needed to do before I was finished.

My geometry notebook also has developed my organizational skills. It is a collection of assignments which is graded as one grade. Because notebooks are checked, I must keep mine organized and make sure to have all of my papers in order and in their correct places. In classes where this isn't done, most of my assignments end up in books or scattered throughout my backpack, locker, room, and such.

Interpretive essays in English also contributed to the development of my organizational skills. In those essays the assignment was to focus entirely on what I was writing about and to create everything on ideas throughout the essay. By writing interpretive essays I learned to organize papers and stay focused on the book as well as to search deeply into what I was writing about so I could understand how the parts of the book functioned together to create the impact of the whole thing.

My leadership skills have become stronger this semester. In most of my classes I have been working in groups for a variety of projects. In English we've worked in groups developing graphics and in geometry we've worked in groups checking homework. One group project in history was quite frustrating, but I managed to lead my group to a fairly good grade. This particular project wasn't very difficult, but the members of my group seemed to have never had any direction in their lives. They seemed all to be working together to accomplish as little as possible. As I struggled to bring some control and focus to the task at hand, I learned that in everything I do there will always be something trying to stop me, and it is my decision whether to let it stop me or not.

Another group experience came in English with the making of an interpretive graphic. In my group we were trying compare *My Antonia* to "Forrest Gump." The assignment was to base our graphic on an idea that the two works had in common and to work from there. Before we had any strong foundation ideas, my group members began thinking about what we were going to do. I had to keep pulling them back into the first step. In the end we came out with a great finished product.

Besides assignments I have also had particular moments which were impactful to my schooling experiences this year. One of those moments reinforced my feeling of organization; the other, my group leadership skills.

The first time I got my geometry notebook graded I was instructed to make a grading sheet with spaces for all the areas which were being checked and to leave a space where I would give myself a grade. I knew I was pretty organized, but I didn't think it was quite what Mrs. Horn expected, so I gave myself a "B." When I got my grade back I had earned an "A" for my effort. I was very proud of my work, and since that time I have been certain to keep all my assignments organized so I can earn an "A" next time as well.

Another moment was in history when we were doing group work. No one in my group seemed to be doing anything, so I asked them why they weren't participating. One of my group members told me they were waiting for me, "their leader," to tell them what to do. I was honored that they looked at me as a leader, but also a bit disappointed in them because they couldn't figure out what to do until someone gave them instructions. Working with groups has been a learning experience about how to develop and use my leadership potential.

During the course of this semester my position in my classes has changed. I began the year feeling like just another student. I didn't care much if I did really well or if I just passed all my classes and could then go on to next year, the year after, and the rest of my life. I wasn't doing poorly; I just wasn't putting forth the energy to live up to my fullest potential. Now, at the end of the first semester, I am getting a 4.0 GPA and am doing all I can to maintain excellent grades. I have taken the leadership role in most group activities I've been involved in and I am more accepting of other people's ideas and contributions as a result. Although school is not very exciting for me, I know I must do my best at it so it will be easier to complete.

Next semester I intend to keep up with my 4.0 GPA and to have a little more fun doing it. I have discovered how much easier it makes my entire life if I am doing well in school.

Angela

Parent's Reply

Dear Angela,

It is with great pride that I have watched your attitude change. You are not only doing better in school as a result of taking more responsibility for yourself and your actions, you are doing better at everything and feeling much better about yourself. The change is obvious to everyone who cares about you. Many people have commented on how much more pride and self-respect you have. Those are characteristics that must be present for a person to maintain a leadership role. Without those characteristics people can't respect you and they have no reason to be led.

I am very proud of your incredible growth this past year. It is great to see you working up to your potential. There is no limit to what you are capable of accomplishing.

Love,

Mom

The imaginary portfolio. While I often use the letter assignment as the end-paper to a formative or a showcase portfolio, I have also used it as an assignment in itself, through which students create an imaginary portfolio, depicting their growth as students by describing selected assignments from across curricular areas without actually including them in a bound portfolio booklet. To compose this letter, students must first establish their own criteria as to what is involved in becoming an effective student. In class we discuss "studentdom," examining the elements that are involved in growing as a student, and brainstorming characteristics of an effective student (e.g., reader, writer, problem-solver, independent learner, creator, class-builder, etc.). As with any portfolio assignment, students determine how they will focus their paper as they discriminate among and evaluate their most profound areas of impact during the period in question. Then again, as in the full portfolio assignment, students return to the folders from all of their classes to revisit specific assignments, activities, and experiences that have affected them as students. In their letters

students include descriptions of three or four product-based assignments, assignments that were graded by the teacher, and they include
descriptions and reflections on selected intangible moments that
were pivotal in their growth as students.

Students address their letters to a specific person outside of our
classroom, and they are required to obtain a written response to
their letter to be included in the portfolio along with it. If the letter
serves as the end-letter to a concrete portfolio, responses often address the portfolio itself as well as the letter. Not only does this process provide students with a chance to see how they are presenting
themselves through their portfolios, it also provides a way for us to
involve the community in the educational process. Through such
interaction with the larger community, students are validated *by* the
community as to the value of what they're doing in school, and the
school is validated *in* the community as it becomes more aware of
the breadth and depth of learning that goes on in our diverse classrooms, the media notwithstanding.

Whereas the specific formative or showcase portfolio that houses this letter and its response might be based on a single discipline
or even a single subject within a discipline, the end-letter will by
definition draw on examples from a variety of disciplines as students explore their growth as learners. Such a process can be
invaluable in helping students break through the compartmentaliza-
tion that is so common in today's schools and remind them of a central reason for being in school: to broaden their perspectives as they
develop the strategies and skills to enable them to be productive
members of society and, in Maslow's words, fully functioning human beings.

Portfolio work means staying open and selecting, taking risks
and revising, sharing and reflecting, accepting and assessing. Portfolio experiences allow students the luxury of revisiting their body
of work, both the processes and the products, of examining it as a
whole to see their growth and change over time. When used in the
classroom, portfolios allow teachers the luxury of individualizing
instruction, as students invite us into their growth processes
through the artifacts they choose to include in their portfolios and
their reasons for including them. And they allow teachers and students both to extend and to validate the role that parents and community members play in education by inviting outside responses to
the portfolio.

The following chart shows how both formative and showcase
portfolios can be used in the classroom. Teachers need to be clear as
to purpose and convey that purpose to students and parents.

FORMATIVE PORTFOLIOS AND SHOWCASE PORTFOLIOS

A chart showing how purpose drives process and shapes final portfolios

FORMATIVE PORTFOLIOS
for classroom or personal use

Purpose: to show student growth or progress in a given area(s); purpose established by student and/ or teacher

Audience: most often known to the portfolio creator, often consisting of peers, teacher, parents, and/or others whom the student may choose

Artifacts: may include pieces of work that the student may not want publicly reviewed—pieces that are appropriate to this portfolio because they offer benchmarks from which growth can be measured or because they represent a turning point in a student's learning, though they may not show a pinnacle of achievement

Structure: arranged according to student/teacher purposes; contains a cover, a table of contents, a preface or introductory letter, selected artifacts, and a final reflective piece; may include artifacts other than written documents, e.g., tapes, graphics, photographs

SHOWCASE PORTFOLIOS
for classroom or large-scale assessment

Purpose: to show student accomplishment in a pre-determined area(s); provides a showcase of work; purpose established externally (by district, state, national assessors, employers, etc.)

Audience: a wider, more public audience than that of the classroom portfolio; audience may consist of people unknown to the portfolio creator

Artifacts: will most likely showcase only the student's best works of required types or evidence of required performances

Structure: arranged according to specifications set up by the assessment body

FORMATIVE PORTFOLIOS
for classroom or personal use

Reflection: focuses on processes in which students engaged as they completed each work and examines their new perceptions as they re-vision it for inclusion in this particular portfolio; helps establish and maintain focus by explaining how each selection adds to the pictures students are building of their growth and learning; includes self-assessment, exploring the degree of participation and the quality of performance represented by each selection; often exploratory in tone, reflective piece may consider how entries show patterns of learning and speculate on direction of future growth

Assessment: external assessment is largely holistic and response-based; focuses on the extent to which students fulfill their stated purpose; may include, in addition to the final reflective piece, a measure of self-assessment threaded throughout; self-assessment is taken into account by those assessing the portfolio as a whole; generally assessment is performed by people known to the portfolio creator

SHOWCASE PORTFOLIOS
for classroom or large-scale assessment

Reflection: focuses on the importance of the required artifacts and/or on how each selection shows evidence of accomplishment; may show how each entry adds to the picture students are creating of themselves; may include some discussion of the processes that went into the final construction of each selection or into the selection process itself

Assessment: external assessment is largely analytical; portfolios are measured against pre-established purposes and externally imposed standards; may be assigned several different scores, reflecting degree of achievement in specific areas (e.g., reading, writing, scientific method, etc.) as well as effectiveness of portfolio as a whole; often assessment is performed by people unknown to the portfolio creator

Adapted from chart by Joan Brown

Chapter Six

Measuring Success
A Department Changes from Within

Moving from external assessment to authentic assessment is just one aspect of totally restructuring the way we think about teaching, which means the way we look at ourselves as well as the way we look at our students. The pressures of being a teacher today loom so large that they may blind us to student change. We are often too busy to be mindful observers as we go about the daily work in our classrooms. Without meaning to, we bend assessment of a student's work to our subjective sense of that student, often labeling Peter as a consistent A student or Jennifer as a B, regardless of the variations that occur in the quality of their work, whatever that means. We continue to see Ricardo as a D student, even though we know that he is a whiz in math, but he hadn't mastered the intricacies of English when he came into our classroom and we haven't noticed that his writing is more fluent and his participation in team projects central to the success of the team. We see what we believe to be true, based on what we bring to the assessment—our biases, prejudices, and preconceptions, as well as our own experience as students. We bring our predilections in how we learn, how we process information to bear as we assess how students go about their work. All this goes on even as we may think we are grading a paper objectively, according to preset standards of conventions, structure, and diction. But we mustn't be too hard on ourselves. We *are* busy. We *are* overworked. But we can learn to step back from our selves and look with new eyes.

What we can learn to do: Be mindful observers. We can observe students talking, writing, listening. Jot down what we observe as we go. Learn to look at purpose as we assess every aspect of the student's performance—the journals, the logs, the collaborative efforts, the graphics, the speaking, the final products. Give lots of feedback along the way, but learn to withhold final judgment until we have a body of work, a portfolio, available for a reflective assessment. Teach students the practice of self-evaluation and learn to trust it. Help them learn to trust it. There is no need for pop quizzes or multiple-choice reading comprehension questions in the classroom of the teacher who practices the new paradigm. Alice Roy, writing in *College English*, notes that "Destructive, or unconstructive, practices may persist because an unconscious assessment of the curriculum and pedagogy suggests that things are good enough, or about as good as they are going to get. Theory, then, itself often unconscious, but always present, is reinforced, and so skills-based, handbook-driven writing courses, for example, . . . may continue unquestioned."[1]

Questioning is, perhaps, the first step toward awareness, and awareness the first step toward change. While reform begins with individual change, it can be speeded up, focused, and implemented in a school setting when a group of people—a grade level or whole faculty of an elementary school or a department in a middle or high school—work together over time. Most of us have participated many times in department reviews or school accreditation studies that result in newly phrased objectives and goals. They are written up, admired, then filed. There is no time for the staff development that would result in implementing our lofty goals. Few of us, I think, have been involved in a restructuring event so fundamental to the way an entire department reconceptualizes itself as that which took place in a middle school in a small town in what John Steinbeck referred to as "The Pastures of Heaven," Salinas, California. To tell the story of the teachers at this school, I am turning over the first person narrative to Kelly Smith, the high school teacher who, above all, enabled the transformation. The model has been created: what happened at this school can happen at others.

Department Change from Within

Kelly Smith

It is a rare and wondrous thing when teachers have an opportunity to work together to produce something unified and meaningful. It is even more wondrous knowing that what one group of teachers did reflects the rich tapestry of talents, styles, and viewpoints that comprise every middle school Language Arts department. While the student population of El Sausal Middle School may be significantly different from that of most schools in the country, its staff is familiar: dedicated, overworked, stressed by the pressures of the society, yet committed to do the best they can for their students. As their coach I have been privileged to observe one of the most exciting processes one can witness, especially as a teacher who is both "within and without" the program. Like Gatsby, I was *with* but not *of* this department.

When I began my relationship with El Sausal and its staff, I was a teacher at the high school across town. I knew very little about El Sausal; my surface knowledge came from the general supposition that this middle school seemed to be facing numerous challenges. The student population, primarily Hispanic, came from the lower socioeconomic group. Many of these students' parents were seasonal or migrant agricultural workers, and almost 75% of the students were identified as limited English Proficient. Every year a great number of teachers resigned and new teachers were hired. It was a good place to get experience before moving on. The enormous turnover combined with the number of "at risk" and language minority students made developing an articulated program extremely difficult.

Even though El Sausal's challenges were demanding, a core group of teachers at this school were doing remarkable things. The Language Development staff was knowledgeable, some known throughout the state for their bilingual education expertise. The Reading and English teachers were dedicated and willing to develop their programs. So in the spring of 1990, when the opportunity to write a Middle School Demonstration Program grant became available, these teachers were willing to jump into the turbulent sea of change. Before I begin this successful sea story, however, I feel there are some important lessons we learned that should be pointed out. I offer this list of what I now see to be critical features for change so I can point out the places where we took the correct course to program development and where we took the detours that led away from our destination. Of course I'll also offer our key learnings and epiphanies along the way.

Critical Features for Change

- **Creating team spirit: Developing a sense of community.**
  When we began to be successful in developing our program we were working as a team, spending time together, breaking down the walls. We were creating a sense of collaboration, sharing

strategies, feeling that the whole is greater than the parts. Moving from a state of competition to a state of collaboration empowered our teachers to attempt difficult classroom strategies and techniques. New teachers were embraced by the group and in turn embraced the goals and objectives that had been developed during previous years. New and experienced teachers were meeting informally at lunch to share ideas and discuss difficulties. For many teachers this lunch-time "training" was key to feeling like a part of a strong, respected department. With no steering committee, everyone became a stakeholder.

- **Having a goal.** Having a clear goal allowed us to channel our energies: We became obsessed with the work of our department. By putting energy into one group, we created a driving force. As the department became stronger and more focused, it became the critical mass for schoolwide change. As we clarified our goal, we were able to establish the criteria by which we would measure our success.

- **Outside eyes: Seeing ourselves through the eyes of others.** Each member of a department sees from a unique perspective. This is both powerful, as it opens the way for discussion and self-assessment, and limiting, as it isolates members in their own rooms with their own ideas. Ultimately, we need to see ourselves through the eyes of others and allow for their input and feedback. In our case, we began by asking only "friends" to come into our private worlds, our classrooms. But as time went on, the outside eyes became those of another teacher from El Sausal, a teacher from another school in our district, a site or district administrator, or a visitor from another city. As members of a team, our teachers were supported from within when outsiders would wander through the classes. Both the positive and negative program reviews gave us the impetus to continue our change process.

- **Coaching: Providing internal and external leadership.** Everyone needs help in implementing the changes in curriculum and instruction that the group has agreed on. Having an administrator who understands the plan and supports it with released time, encouragement, and recognition is critical. You can't build team spirit if only a few can attend a meeting. Along with administrative support, teachers needed help with the nitty-gritty aspects of changing instructional practices. Where do we get the butcher paper and what literature supports our themes became questions for the coach. The coach was not only ready with markers, scissors, glue, and ideas, but also available for team planning of units and team teaching of lessons, a willing participant in classroom instruction.

- **Events.** Getting ready for an event is critical to the process of change. If there is no event, there seems to be no reason to change. Even for our students, preparing for a "publication " event—the process of taking a piece from pre-writing to publication, or research to oral presentation—is more important than the final moment of completion. The event gives us impetus to complete the process. The product is gratifying in its own right, but the learning occurs throughout the process.

With these features in mind, the story begins—without me, as I was not yet involved. A core group of teachers at El Sausal planned and wrote their first Middle School Demonstration Program grant. Their three-year plan included interdisciplinary teams, thematically tying the English core curriculum with the Social Studies curriculum. They also envisioned a school where writing was used as a tool for learning in all classes and a school that would become, in the words of the grant application, a "print-rich environment where reading is seen not only as a tool for learning but as an enjoyable, fulfilling pastime." Their goal was to use the grant to produce schoolwide change, "where the artificial boundaries between content areas will begin to fade, where students actively engage with others to create meaning from literature; where students actively interact, in depth, with integrated content and apply what they learn in meaningful contexts; where teachers understand and appreciate the importance of structuring classroom lessons that build and extend on the students' own experience; and where teachers display increased competence in delivering high quality instruction to every student at El Sausal Middle School."

> In retrospect, we see that the plan was too ambitious from the beginning. I now believe that to change a program, we need to start with one group and move out to the greater whole. By looking for schoolwide change, this first plan was too difficult and ultimately unattainable. Later, when we focused on a single group, they would find success and ultimately affect the entire school by example.

The Middle School Demonstration Program awarded El Sausal fifty thousand dollars for the next three years. Ann Jaramillo, the primary grant writer and an incredibly talented teacher at the school, became the site coordinator and began planning for the first year of grant implementation.

My involvement with El Sausal began when, as a teacher-consultant for both the area writing and literature projects, I conducted a series of Wednesday night workshops for English and social studies/history teachers. We were to focus on reading and writing across-the-curriculum strategies. Ann convinced the entire English and Reading staffs (there were two separate departments at this point) and the majority of the Social Science department to attend these workshops. It's hard to imagine, but the teachers chose to work at night rather than to miss their classes! This is the kind of dedication that pervades the corridors of El Sausal. The sessions went from 4 P.M. to 9 P.M. and took place in the staff lounge, making it convenient for teachers to attend. Additionally, Ann ordered a specially catered dinner for each session. Many of the teachers commented that although they had been absolutely exhausted when they arrived for the training, they were revitalized by the time the session was over. Here they had a chance to meet and interact with their colleagues in a way that they rarely had experienced. The training consisted of the teachers learning by experiencing the techniques and strategies much as students would.

In retrospect, the way we began this process was absolutely perfect. This beginning step was critical for establishing a sense of camaraderie and team spirit. This training also proved to teachers that this program would be different from most staff development workshops: teachers were paid for the training time and were served a wonderful dinner in the middle of the session. Years later, teachers have said that the money was not why they went to the session, but that they appreciated having their time valued with these kinds of outward signs.

After six weeks of training, Ann felt confident that the teachers were ready to implement the newly learned strategies in their classrooms. The next step was trying to get teachers to begin involving themselves in peer coaching.

*It didn't work. The workshop had given them the beginning of community and trust, but they were not ready to put themselves into that kind of vulnerable position. Looking back, they see that although they had an awareness of constructivist thinking and student-centered approaches, they weren't yet grounded enough in the philosophy and strategies to effect immediate changes in their teaching. It is interesting that we all made the assumption that since the teachers really had responded positively to the training, they were already using these strategies in their classrooms. The ones who were, were mostly those who had already been using these strategies anyway. Most had not yet made any changes in how they taught reading or writing. These teachers were not used to having others in their classrooms and had no desire to put themselves in a vulnerable position. **Our first lesson: fundamental classroom change takes time, and support needs to come from a neutral outsider**. It's too scary to have a colleague in your classroom.*

The next year rolled around and the grant-implementation committee continued to meet. Teachers went to conferences, and additional training was provided on campus. In the early spring, we hired Fran Claggett to do a two-day workshop on using graphics to deepen student understanding of text. Fran's workshop was wonderfully received. The teachers valued the information she presented, but more than that, they deeply appreciated Fran's style and teaching wisdom. This two-day event began a relationship with Fran that was to last to our present stage in the project.

> *In retrospect, I think it is incredibly important to have an outside consultant that works with a group through the duration of the project. Fran's participation in this effort was significant because she provided a trusted outside eye as well as continued to refresh the group with valued new ideas. When a department has one outside consultant who conducts periodic staff development workshops and makes individual classroom visits, the teachers build up a level of trust and acceptance impossible to achieve with multiple, one-shot, outside consultants.*

Throughout that second year, Ann continued to encourage teachers to participate in peer coaching. Because the coaching component was too unsuccessful, Ann and I decided to create a written resource with the strategies to which the teachers were introduced in the evening workshop series. We thought if the teachers had written descriptions of the strategies and blackline masters, they would be more likely to create lessons using these techniques. So we created graphic organizers, wrote descriptions of the strategies, and gave them student samples to be used as models. That really didn't work either.

> *In retrospect, this was a great idea that didn't work until we provided model lessons and coaching to support the strategies. A few years later, one teacher told me that one of her trigger events for change was when I ran off 150 copies of the blackline masters and just put them in her mail box. She said she tried the strategy only because it was easily accessible. Once she had tried one strategy, it was easier to try others and to begin planning with them in mind.*

When the next year rolled around, another factor began to undermine the change process. A new middle school was to open the following summer. The new school's planning team created some very innovative programs, including built-in teacher collaboration time, a year-round schedule, and a cross-curricular, family-house structure. Additionally, a well-respected administrator was hired to be the principal. Many of the teachers giving leadership to the El Sausal grant were thinking of transferring to the new school. By springtime, the momentum for implementing the grant was fairly well stalled.

When the Middle School Demonstration Program evaluators arrived in April of the second year, they observed very little change in the instructional program at El Sausal. The English, Reading, and History teachers participating in the grant were surprised by the less-than-positive evaluation. In fact, we were incredibly disappointed and more than a little embarrassed. My relationship with the school was still that of workshop presenter and coach, but I was feeling quite involved with the teachers at this point. In May I was invited to a meeting that gave me some insights into the evaluation. First, we didn't understand how to demonstrate our program to an outside audience. We hadn't fully instituted a portfolio system, so the evaluators had very little notion of what students were really doing in the classes. And when the evaluators did understand what was happening in the classes, they were seeing a very skills-oriented program. Additionally, we had lessened our impact on language development and literacy by trying to make the program a cross-curricular effort. I learned that we needed to focus only on those instructors teaching English (mainstream, English as a Second Language, or Special Education) or Reading (for students achieving two years below grade level on standardized tests.) And we needed to learn how to show what our program looks like to an outside audience.

At the end of the year, Candy McCarthy, a special projects coordinator at El Sausal, arranged for a day away from school to reflect on the grant report and to plan for the next year. Candy, Fran, and I (Ann Jaramillo was one of the teachers who had chosen to transfer to the new school) met with the staff who would remain at El Sausal the following year. This meeting was great for team spirit. We were in a wonderful environment, a house on the beach, and we talked about where we were lacking and what we might do the following year. Candy and Fran facilitated and recorded ideas on chart paper, but primarily we just shared our hopes for the following year.

In retrospect, we didn't come up with anything substantive during this meeting. Basically we spent good time together, created some dreams, and healed a few wounds resulting from a poor evaluation and the separation of those going to the new school.

During the summer, Candy and I met several times to develop a strategy for putting the change process in motion the following year. One strategy we devised was that I would be released from my high school classroom two hours a day to work exclusively with the English, Reading, ESL, and Special Education teachers. Candy also managed to get every one of these teachers to sign up for a three-day workshop that I would lead during the first three days of school the following September.

*In retrospect, this was the event that changed us from a disap-
pointed team that had lost an important game to a team willing to
get on the field again.*

During our three-day workshop, we took the broad goals of the
project and the State Language Arts Framework and agreed on five
specific objectives:

- implementation of all aspects of the writing process, from brainstorming through revision to a final published piece
- implementation of all aspects of the reading process, developing
  a language-rich reading program that encourages students to
  read for academic as well as recreational purposes
- implementation of an assessment program that reflects the State
  Language Arts Framework and district curriculum and informs
  students, parents, and teachers about the quality of student performance
- full implementation of the district language arts curriculum, building on a core-literature program wherein students are responsible for creating their own meaning from the adopted texts
- integration of technology into the language arts program, especially for writing and reading process activities

We agreed that the key to success would be to get our students to
read, so one of our first activities was to implement a schoolwide Silent Sustained Reading Program. In order to implement SSR, we pur-
chased enough motivational reading material to provide materials for
every classroom at El Sausal.

*In retrospect, this was a really important turning point. We included
the entire staff in our effort, asking them to support our cause, but
also offering materials to enable the support to be easily given.*

Another important idea emerging from our three days together was
that we should meet once a week, on Wednesdays, to continue discussing how to implement our goals and objectives. We decided that
the project was important enough to meet often to evaluate our
progress. The grant paid for the teachers' time when participating in the
Wednesday meetings. Additionally we developed a reading and writing
assessment, using the CLAS format (see Integrated Reading and Writing prompt in Chapter Seven), to evaluate our students with a pre- and
post-assessment. We chose this authentic assessment tool so that we
could evaluate whether our instructional choices were truly making a
difference in student achievement. After these three days together our
team of teachers was beginning to build the kind of community necessary to make significant changes in the school's instructional program.

In retrospect, these three days were extremely important. We no longer had a steering committee making decisions which then had the job of getting others to buy in. Now everyone was a key player in the decision-making process and everyone had a stake in the plan.

We explored how the work students produced could be used to show what our program looked like to an outside observer. These early meetings were really the first time that the strategies learned in our evening workshops, a year and a half earlier, were treated as viable options for use in the classroom. As one of our objectives stated that students should be responsible for creating their own meaning from our district-adopted core texts, we tried to give examples of strategies that would result in this kind of student performance. During the fall, these strategies slowly began to make their way into instruction. For example, the Reading teachers began using strategies such as the Dialectical Journal when getting ready for short story discussions. We also tried to establish how we could format a writing process activity that would help the outside observer understand just what stages the students go through to get to a published piece of writing. Ultimately these discussions led to a fully developed portfolio assessment system. Our portfolios showcase examples of student work that reflect our program objectives.

During the same period that we were meeting on Wednesdays, I began visiting classes every day. Often I would only spend 10 or 15 minutes in each class, rarely giving anything but positive feedback. My primary goal was to establish trust and to allow the teachers to feel supported by the program. However, another goal was to help the teachers see their own instructional program through the eyes of an outsider. Soon, the teachers and the students began to feel comfortable with other adults in the classrooms.

A few weeks before Thanksgiving, one of the key events for propelling the effort along took place. The teachers asked me to go to each classroom and evaluate it as if I were a Middle School Demonstration Project Evaluator. I was worried about doing this because I didn't want to be in an evaluative position with the staff, yet I knew it was a wonderful opportunity to give them some much-needed feedback about the program. Because of my concern for completing these visits in a sensitive way, I decided to develop a tool that would focus the entire visit on student evidence. My first "evidence check sheet" was a one-page, double-column document. In the left column I wrote the objectives we had created and added a few categories that are at the heart of our State English–Language Arts framework. In each of these categories I listed the student work (and classroom strategies) that might be used to illuminate the objectives. Across from each of these catagories was a space in the right-hand column for me to record the student evidence I observed when I visited each classroom. My first mock visitation was very successful. When I observed student work that reflected our objectives, I recorded what I saw on the evidence check sheet. When evidence was not present, I simply wrote "no evidence present." At the end of my visit in each classroom, I handed the "Evidence Check" to the teacher. After school on the mock visitation day, all of the teachers and I met. I explained that if I wrote "no evidence present" it didn't mean that the teacher hadn't done the activities; it just meant that I couldn't see it in the student work present on the walls or in the portfolios.

> *In retrospect, this simple document is probably the most important tool we've developed to implement and evaluate our program. The one-page design makes it easy to use and the information is simply displayed. It also made the entire program easy to view at a glance. The fact that I gave it to the teachers after the visit was also quite successful. Later, as we progressed in our development, I used a single sheet to record evidence from all classrooms and published it for each teacher. By doing one for the entire program, we could share ways of evidencing the objectives and see the strengths and weaknesses of the whole program.*

In December we took our evidence check concept to another level. We invited Fran, who had already worked with the staff several times, to participate in an innovative peer coaching event. Each staff member was paired with someone with whom they felt comfortable working. In the space of two days, each teacher was observed teaching by their partner and by Fran. After each lesson, Fran and the two teachers debriefed the observation and used the evidence check sheet to create future lesson plans. Even though this event was a logistical nightmare, it was fully supported by the principal, Abel Valdez, and his secretary, who scheduled the substitutes. Because this unique kind of peer coaching was facilitated by Fran, the post-conferences were informative and extremely valuable.

> *In retrospect, this event was another powerful agent for change. Fran played the role of the "outside eye," yet was a trusted member of our greater community. She provided insights into our developing instruction and suggested new strategies to further our efforts.*

Note from the author: As an outside visitor to the El Sausal classrooms, I was one of the "events" to help prepare teachers for outside evaluators. I was one step removed from Kelly, who had become such a constant visitor and coach in the classrooms that she was completely nonthreatening. They knew me, but only as an outside consultant who lived two hundred miles away. So when I visited their classrooms with the check sheet in hand, their level of anxiety went up. The form worked admirably. I could circulate around the class-room, read the walls, look at student folders, note classroom libraries, observe students at work, either individually or in teams—all without interfering with the work of the day. The students were used to Kelly's visits; they noticed me, but only in a peripheral way. They were ex-traordinarily polite, offering me their work to look at when I asked and answering any questions I had about what they were doing.

The Evidence Check Sheet can be used by teacher visitors, ad-ministrators, outside evaluators, or by the teachers themselves. Posted on the classroom wall, it allows students to participate in the assessment process, to be able to monitor their own learning. A classroom with a lot of books around, with student work—drawings, poems, essays—on the walls, with folders and beginning portfolios filed by class but easily accessible—these are signs of an active learning environment and are immediately apparent.

I recommend this form, or some such form, to all teachers as a means of self-assessment as well as evaluations by others. Imagine: You could give this form to your principal the next time you are being evaluated! It might preclude the situation I found myself in one year when my principal came around for the required evaluation visits: Finding my students working in teams doing a variety of tasks, she noted that she would come back later, "when you are teaching." This scenario was repeated twice more, then she gave up. Unfortunately, many of our administrators need this kind of awareness training as much as we do. Now, back to Kelly's story.

After winter break, the teachers became more and more motivated to get ready for the MSDP evaluators, who would conduct the final evaluation in April. During the months of January, February, and March, Fran visited the classrooms for a second time. In preparation of the for-mal evaluation, the site adminstrators and finally a group of district adminstrators visited classrooms. Each team of visitors was trained to use the Evidence Check Sheet before they entered our classrooms. The teachers knew exactly when they would be visited and understood that these visits were not part of their formal evaluations. If a teacher was overwhelmed by the amount of work involved in getting ready for these events, I used grant money for release time, during which they could plan their lesson or develop necessary materials. Our Wednes-day meetings continued and we began meeting in a different room ev-ery week, giving all teachers the opportunity to show off their rooms.

During this period, my role was completely one of support. One teacher told me that she was willing to have students work in groups to create collaborative posters, but just didn't quite know how to do it. I walked to the work room, pulled sheets of butcher paper off the roll, cut them up, and folded them into squares. Then I brought my class-room marking pens into the room. Once the tools for the activity were present, the teacher fully embraced the activity and has been using these kinds of strategies since that time.

Our last major push occurred two days before the grant evalua-tors were to arrive. We had a district staff development day to pre-pare for the evaluation. I gave the teachers the entire morning to work in their rooms, with the understanding that as a group we would visit each room in the afternoon. Each teacher was given a lesson plan page to complete and was to be ready to explain what they would be doing on the evaluation day. Again the visits would focus on the student work and the evidence of our objectives.

In retrospect, this event was very important. Everyone knew what the criteria for success were, and because the community had become strong, everyone wanted to be successful for the rest of the team. It was also incredibly important for each person to have a feeling for what the whole program looked like to the outsiders.

When the evaluation day came, we were ready. We met in the morning with the evaluators and our site and district adminstrators, giv-ing them the broad picture of the program. After this meeting, the evaluation team went to each English, Reading, ESL, and Special Edu-cation classroom looking for the evidence of a quality English–Lan-guage Arts program. In the classrooms, they saw evidence of students working together, students using graphics to enhance their understand-ing of the text, students using technology to work though the writing process, students involved in many writing domains, and student work blanketing the walls. When they left we had a very big party!

We knew we wouldn't know the outcome of the evaluation for months, and, ironically, two of the most important changes happened after the evaluation. Because of the enormous amount of collabora-tion between the English, ESL, Reading, and Special Education de-partments, teachers began to discuss the possiblity of changing to an integrated Reading and English program, giving every student in the school a two-hour block of "language arts." Reading teachers, whose curriculum had been very skills-oriented, had begun using many of the student-centered strategies to help students interact with text. English teachers were willing to adopt the Great Books Reading pro-gram and integrate it with the district-adopted core literature. These discussions were taking place at the same time as the entire staff was creating a schoolwide vision statement.

In May, Candy McCarthy and Abel Valdez arranged for a critical event to take place. The entire school participated in our post-assessment. Every teacher in the school adminstered our authentic reading and writing assessment in the morning, and in the afternoon the entire staff participated in scoring the reading section of the assessment. I was really nervous about training the staff to score the reading, so I took advantage of my extensive familiarity with large-scale scoring and set it up the way I would a CLAS reading. Our Language Arts teachers were table leaders and the rest of the staff were trained as readers. I had each teacher score his or her own homeroom students. This scoring event was another link in the chain that led the staff to develop a schoolwide literacy goal.

> In retrospect, this was another powerful event. Because teachers were scoring their own students, they gained insights into their students' reading process. For some, the CLAS scoring guides described reading in terms that they had not heard before and gave the teachers a new understanding of what reading performances looked like. Many teachers said that they didn't know their students could do the kind of work that was evidenced in this assessment. Because of the cohesiveness that led to the development of the schoolwide literacy goal, the staff was willing to consider a new school schedule. The new rotating schedule included two-hour language arts blocks while allowing for a stronger elective program, rather than eliminating electives.

We ended the year knowing that something very special and significant had taken place at El Sausal. The Language Arts teachers were a powerful community, having created a language-rich environment for their students.

During the summer, we received our evaluation and found that we had not been awarded an MSDP grant. Though we were disappointed, we were too committed to our new program to allow the disappointment to stop the development. The momentum was still strong. Teachers had gained the internal sense of the power of what they were doing. The transfer of power from outside evaluator to inside knowledge is, perhaps, the most significant result of the evaluators' report.

The next year began with two-hour language arts blocks and electives for every student at El Sausal. These two goals were accomplished by adding an extra period in the schedule (a total of seven periods) and rotating the schedule through five periods on any given day. The other content teachers loved the schedule because their total minutes per period were increased but fewer classes were taught each day. Because teachers only taught five periods out of any seven, they also had more planning time. With the lengthened periods and two-period blocks, Language Arts teachers were thrilled with the caliber of student work. The evidence on the walls and in portfolios was even richer than it had been the year before. (See Portfolio Assessment guidelines at the end of this chapter.)

Early that fall, we took the final report from the MSDP and used the commendations and recommendations to write a new plan for the year. We had enough carryover money to have Fran back several times, nourishing the community we had worked so hard to develop. Additionally, the district was so impressed with El Sausal's success that they wanted to create the same kind of program at the other two district middle schools. My afternoon job at El Sausal turned into that of a full-time resource teacher position with responsibilities at all three middle schools.

Using the lessons learned at El Sausal, I began employing the same strategies with Washington and Harden middle schools. Each school used the MSDP self-study to evaluate their current program and to write a language arts plan. District staff development time was utilized to provide inservice for each of these schools. Soon, I began spending more time in classrooms, team planning and teaching lessons. The tricky issue at Harden and Washington was to get the same kind of commitment without the grant money or the goal of getting ready for an outside evaluator. To counteract this challenge, we brought in many "outside eyes" and tried to create a program unique to each school. At the cornerstone of all of these efforts is the "Evidence Check" built on the state framework and our district's vision of a student-centered, language-rich program. Currently this program is being expanded to include a History Resource teacher, Cindy Lenners, and is gently being nudged into the high school programs in our district. This effort is supported by our Superintendant, Aurora Quevedo, our Assistant Superintendant, Roger Anton, and the Title One Director, Mike McGraw.

At Harden Middle School, teacher commitment to interdisciplinary teaming and sheltered instruction for LEP students allowed the administration to bring in a remarkable trainer, Aida Walqui. The entire staff has received six days of specialized inservice regarding the issues associated with special needs students. Each of the teachers implemented this training by team planning and team teaching a unit with one of the resource teachers or by writing interactive journals about the experience of sheltering instruction. To the credit of this dedicated staff, most teachers chose the team teaching option, which gave us a rare opportunity to work collaboratively in developing lessons and strategies that can be shared with the entire district. It has also given staff members an opportunity to try strategies that were foreign to them before the inservice.

The Harden staff has begun planning the follow-up training for next years' School Improvement Days. They will focus on interdisciplinary teaching with an emphasis on sheltering instruction. During this time, Cindy Lenners and I brought the English and History departments together to write an interdisciplinary grant for the Middle School Demonstration Project. Because both the Language Arts and Social Studies teachers embraced the strategies learned at El Sausal, the MDSP awarded an interdisciplinary grant to Harden.

Originally, striving to get the MSDP grant was an important reason for the El Sausal teachers to change. It wasn't, however, until we got the less-than-positive evaluation that we had a concrete, articulated focus. Once our goal became clear and our community solid, important changes began to take place. The Evidence Check made the criteria for change accessible to everyone, and the outside eyes gave us a mirror in which to see ourselves more clearly. Each event gave us a common experience and the momentum to move toward a unified, meaning-centered, language-rich environment for our students. Although this project began with the Language Arts teachers at El Sausal, the Salinas Union High School District has embraced this vision and continues to strive toward creating a quality program for all students in our district.

Evidence Check List for Classroom Evaluators

Criteria to Show Evidence of Student Learning	Notations of Evidence Present: Comments
1. Coreworks Evidence that shows students interacting with the district-adopted coreworks, e.g., book posters, written work on characters, graphics showing understanding of themes in coreworks, etc.	
2. Supplemental Reading Supplemental reading materials available to students through classroom libraries. Evidence might include student projects, reading logs, reading journals, book reports, etc.	
3. Writing Process/Activities Evidence of students working through stages to a final written work, e.g., brainstorming, prewriting strategies, clustering, peer response groups, revision activities. Variety of written activities and kinds of writing evident. Editing activities leading to publication.	
4. Student-Centered Learning Evidence of students creating their own understanding of text and themes of the core curriculum. Evidence might include graphics, dialectical journals, reading logs, individual and collaborative projects.	
5. Collaborative Speaking/Listening Evidence of collaboration to enhance understanding in literature or skills in writing. Multiple names on projects, peer response in writing, oral/aural project evaluations, student desks clustered together all show collaboration.	
6. Reading Process/Graphics Evidence of students developing an understanding of text through multiple interactions with the text. Graphic responses, logs, writing responses, collaborative activities, text re-creations, authentic assessments show reading process.	
7. Multimedia/Technology Evidence of students engaging in a variety of technologies and media to enhance reading, writing, speaking, and listening skills. Evidence includes word processing, video productions, hypercard presentations, telecommunication research, etc.	
8. Portfolios/Assessment Evidence of students engaging in authentic assessments such as integrated, performance-based assessments, open-ended questions, rubric-based writing, project-based assessments, portfolio collections, introductions, self-assessments.	

Portfolio Assessment Guidelines

El Sausal Middle School Language Arts Program

The purposes of the Language Arts Portfolio Assessment at
El Sausal Middle School are

1. to involve students in self-reflection and evaluation
2. to encourage student self-esteem by valuing their own work
3. to show/track growth and progress over time
4. to report information regarding individual student growth to students, parents, and staff
5. to create a systematic assessment of articulated Curriculum 7–12
6. to showcase student work for review by other teachers, parents, and members of the larger community (show portfolios will be passed from grade to grade).

All Language Arts Show Portfolios at El Sausal during the 1994–95 school year will include

1. Pre-Post Integrated Assessment (7th and 8th)
2. Timed/Pressure Writing on any topic
3. Process Piece of Writing (any topic)
4. Response to Core (other than writing)
5. Favorite Piece (any piece)
6. Booklist (a record of the books read over the year)

In addition to the above requirements, each show portfolio will include

1. color-coordinated entry slip for each student submission
2. an introduction to the entire portfolio (Dear Reader/Resume)
3. color-coordinated table of contents for the year's selections

Other components:

1. Each teacher will keep a storage portfolio for all student work (storage portfolios will not be passed).
2. Students will have the opportunity to conference with teachers about the work they are selecting for the show portfolios.
3. Folders will be provided for both storage and show portfolios.

Optional components:

1. The cover of the show portfolios will have student work displayed (self-portraits, mandalas, poetry, etc.).
2. Students will have the opportunity to include projects in their show portfolios.

Chapter Seven

In Large Measure
School, District, and State Assessment

Grading and Assessment

The actual "giving" of grades hasn't received much direct regard in this book, even though report cards are the driving force behind most teachers' attention to assessment. Report cards loom large every six or nine weeks, forcing us to confront our grading system. Do we have enough grades? Can we support the grades by convoluted mathematical computations? Will students be upset with their grades? Will parents? If we were all adept at keeping logs and notations of student learning, if we had a structure that would help us do that, if we had portfolios! The fact is, most of us do have to fill out report cards, no matter what else we're doing. Some few schools and some brave teachers, however, are conjuring up alternatives, even without sanction of whole-school reform. In the vignette that follows, you will read the words of such a teacher—an outrageously creative, focused, demanding, caring fifth-grade teacher who instituted her own report card reform. In her own words, here is Lynda Chittenden's account of a burning issue.

Report Cards: A Burning Issue
(A narrative account of one teacher's struggle)

by Lynda Chittenden

The flames, fueled by an overgenerous splash of starter fluid, shot up higher than I'd anticipated. I had considered fire-codes and the fact that every year the Fire Marshall dings me about something—too many extension cords stretched from one of the two wall plugs in this tiny classroom, built in 1939, but which now needs to accommodate four computers, aquarium pumps and lights, an electric typewriter, etc. Previous Fire Marshals have also reacted humorlessly to the narrow, cluttered aisles, which are the only space left after seven tables, each seating four students, are grouped around a central rug.

But, the small and dirty portable Bar-B-Que I'd dug out of the basement at home had, I fervently hoped, been rendered safe by the layers of aluminium foil I'd placed both inside and underneath. Nonetheless, the flames continued to crackle and burn, fueled by all the bits of torn paper, and smoke spiraled up towards the ceiling. My entire 5th-grade class, sitting and crouching on the rug, gathered 'round the Bar-B-Que, all strained to see. The flames began to diminish somewhat as the ritualistically torn 29 pieces of what had once been a report card gradually turned into harmless ash. In the uncharacteristic silence, now perfumed by smoke and warmed by the Indian Summer heat of this September afternoon, kids' eyes widened and smiles lit their faces.

Breaking the silence, I quietly said, "All those feelings of failure and memories of disappointment you talked about are also going up in smoke." Some kids' eyes actually followed the upward path of the now thankfully dwindling plume of smoke.

Then, fuel consumed, the fire went out, but the silence remained. Pointing to a list on the board, I asked if anyone would speak aloud, naming one characteristic they knew should be their goal for this school year. One of the very first students called upon, a shy girl who rarely speaks up in class and often appears terrified of attention, quietly said, "Taking risks. . . . I know I need to do that." Next a boisterous and sometimes insensitive boy, a wry grin upon his face, said, "Yeah, I know. . . . I need to respect and work more effectively with others." The kids were amazing, every one of them appropriately chose the goal I would have suggested had I been asked.

Thus, with one activity I'd gotten their attention, introduced the eight Characteristics of a Successful Learner that our school staff had recently identified and defined, as well as announced that this year, we'd have another way to report their school achievements to parents, Discursive Reports, an idea picked up at an Assessment Workshop given by Terry Johnson. Unfortunately, all the necessary political groundwork had not been laid. A cheerfully enthusiastic letter sent home to parents outlining the upper-grade staff's plan to discard the old report card in favor of piloting discursive reports reached a board member before the Superintendent had been briefed. A bit of *merde* hit the fan, resulting in a decree from on high that we could pilot what-ever we wanted, but that we would also use the old report card!

In December, the four 4th- and 5th-grade teachers spent untold hours first writing lengthy, 150+-word discursive reports wherein we explained in explicit detail each child's academic strengths and needed areas of improvement as well as their progress towards at-taining those Successful Learner Characteristic goals. Then, we filled out the old report card for each student wherein a variety of summative marks were used to report achievement. When I ruefully explained to my kids what had happened, that despite the fact we'd burned one, a report card *would* go home, they simply shrugged, and accepted it. (I hoped it wasn't to them another example of adults promising one thing and doing another.) The experiment was a valient, yet futile, effort. The parents were happy, but the discursive report was perceived primarily as an extension of the graded report card, rather than a replacement for it.

So, in March, at the end of the second trimester, I decided to drop both kinds of report cards and instead pilot another idea I'd gotten from the Terry Johnson workshop, Student-Led Conferences. Enough political work had now been done that no furor was raised. The kids eagerly accepted the challenge of preparing for a parent conference that *they* would run alone. Since it would be held during class time, and other conferences would probably also be concurrently taking place, I would only be able to observe them from afar. I would not be a participant. Two letters were sent home informing parents of what we were doing as well as detailing their role and how to behave. Perhaps one would have been enough, but as we talked in class, several of the kids expressed fears of being "grilled" by their parents.

Preparations began with each child making a folder upon which was glued a photo I'd taken of him or her seriously at work in class. A list of the expected contents of this folder was handed out, and the cri-teria for selection discussed. Each kid had the final say on what was to be included, and they were both free and encouraged to choose only the "good stuff." The kids pored through their "Literacy" and "Problem-Solving" Portfolios which, in reality, had been little more than storage folders up to now. I stressed that since this was the end of the second trimester, only work done during that time period should rightfully be selected. A few students couldn't find enough "good" work that was done between December and March, and so had to include some bits done in the fall. We talked about the implications of that.

I'd asked the kids to attach an "analysis sheet" to each selection, but hadn't made out a form. One boy made up his own, which was quickly xeroxed for others to use. So then what everyone wrote for each paper or project included: "what was hard . . . , why I was proud . . . , what I learned . . . ," *and* "extra information . . . ," usually the context or purpose of that assignment. They rehearsed their conferences by going over their folders with their Table Partners.

I'd asked the students to "jot down several specific examples of you having/being something from our list of 'Characteristics of a Successful Learner' . . . the more specific you can make them, the more astounded your parents will be." Several kids taped 4" x 6" index cards to their desk and began their lists. Here's one from another girl who'd chosen risk-taking as her primary goal, although her specifics include other "successful student characteristics": "Gave an answer in history . . . I came to the rug when asked . . . I took a risk and told how and what happened when I sold a magazine . . . I'm keeping eye-contact all the time . . . I worked all the period and didn't give up. . ." etc.

We scheduled four afternoons for the conferences, and all but two parents were able to come to class and conference with their kids during that time (unlike the half-days of released time in October when most parents instead want their parent conference in the early mornings or evenings). Moms and Dads took off work to be there; one boy even had *four* parents present, two birth-parents and two step-parents! (He'd had to make four cups of tea, decorate a special larger table, and was *so* nervous; but he proceeded calmly, even as his mother kept bringing a camera up from her lap and photographing him.) We'd originally scheduled the conferences to last only 15 or 20 minutes, but we soon realized that wasn't enough time. After completing the presentation of their folder, most kids wanted to go back to the computers and show off either their keyboarding abilities or the contents of their word-processing file. And most of the time, the rest of the class was uncharacteristically quiet and focused during those conference afternoons.

Before the conferences, I put two letters in each kid's folder: one, a pep-talk to the student, and the other, a form requesting parent response to our experiment. Here are a few of the parent comments:

> "My daughter's eagerness and excitement about the conference was such a joyful experience for me. The conference allowed her to demonstrate all her skills, and it gave me a true representation of her abilities. I wish we could have done this all along" . . . . "The value of student-led conferences as a self-esteem-building and accountability-encouraging enhancement of the learning process is priceless and well worth the preparation time" . . . "I am very supportive of this type of performance evaluation. My daughter has not only completed the enclosed assignments in a thorough and

thoughtful manner, she is also aware of what she has learned and the purpose of the assignments. She has demonstrated an enthusiasm and ownership of her work that exceeds her commitment in past years. The work she presented in her conference demonstrates a learning process which is exciting and consuming. The conference has given me much more information about her educational progress than a traditional report card ever has" . . . "This is a great step towards responsible actions. By making the students an integral part of the conference, they naturally take more interest in being certain that the work is done well. This is a good way to 'empower' (overused but appropriate word) the students. You have my support" . . . "This was a wonderful idea. It forced our son to really look at his work so far and evaluate it more closely. It also gave us a chance to see and discuss his works, (we usually don't get to see them)" . . . "I've felt for many years that self-esteem is the key to learning. This method of 'reporting to parents' confirms a change in attitude which I strongly support."

Although parents were given the option of receiving further input from me on their child's progress, most said they didn't feel it necessary.

But, the best comments came from the kids. I asked everyone to write me right after their conferences, when they were still flushed with pride and success, and most did. (Since I sometimes refer to myself in the third person as their "sweet" teacher, many letters to me begin with "Dear Sweat Lynda.") Here are some excerpts from those letters:

"I really liked the student-led conferences better than report cards because the kids get to show all their good work as opposed to cramming all the trimester into one little grade. It was kind of hard organizing the papers, but it was easy and made me feel responsible. I really liked all the preparing. I usually get good grades, but I think student-led conferences are more fun" . . . "I prefer these conferences to report cards because it's not just a mark on a piece of paper. Our parents get to see the work" . . . "My parents really loved it too. All week I've been getting compliments about it" . . . "It was a great way to show your parents what you have done over the trimester instead of all your work squeezed into one grade" . . . "I liked the conference better than a report card because you can show your parents what you think is good, not what the teacher thinks about all your work. PS, I like the cookies and tea idea" . . . "It also showed that you trust us in not goofing off and playing around. I liked the responsibility" . . . "When you get a report card, you only have grades and, of course, your parents are proud of you when you get good grades, but they never know exactly *why* you got those grades" . . . "Before the conference I was sort of nervous because I thought they might talk about grades all the time even though you sent out the letters" . . . "I do like the conferences but,

I'd like a report card too next time. I like to see the grades I get. (Also, I get paid!)" . . . "I am happy for the conference because usually my mom sees work I am not proud of, and this time she only saw good work and is proud of me" . . . "I think that you get ten times as much praise than you would with the normal thing."

The value of the student-led conferences was evident to me even before the first conference began: "The atmosphere, the morale, the smiles . . . there has actually been *elation* present as the kids chose and analyzed the contents of their folders, preparing to present this work to you, the most important people in their lives" (March 19, letter to parents). Watching the conferences from around the room, eavesdropping whenever I could, and then reading all the comments merely confirmed what I already knew. The students had taken an active stance regarding accountability for their work, and they had been perceived as enthusiastic and adept beings who can adequately report what they are doing in school, and how well they're doing it!

But, an even more subtle and important value of these conferences was revealed in one letter from a boy I'd begun to despair of *ever* motivating. A very bright kid, he spends most of his school days avoiding and/or rushing through work so that "done," he can socialize or go back to the Dungeons and Dragons manuals he adores. His letter was terse and intriguing: "The student-led conference was ok. It wasn't what I planned it to be, but we can't be picky, can we? I liked it because it allowed me to explain my work, and not have it stuffed into one little letter. Another thing is that I could let my parents see good things. The bad thing is it didn't go the way I planned." (He was one who'd had to go all the way back to September to find enough "good stuff" for his folder.) When asked why it hadn't gone the way he'd anticipated, he actually said to me, "I wish I'd done more good work, then I'd have had more to show. If I'd really understood what this was, *I might have worked harder.*" (The italics are mine!)

A year has passed since I wrote the foregoing. That class has gone on to the Middle School, and the boy who "might have worked harder" has in his last trimester of sixth grade finally made the Honor Roll. My experimenting with report cards has continued. This school year my "grade-level mate" and I received permission from our school board to pilot a card with 3 descriptive performance scales from #6 to #1 in Reading, Writing, and Mathematics. After rating each child, the rest of the report card contained a long discursive report. We weren't required to include summative grades on anything.

We began the year with at least one goal being negotiated and then selected at an October conference of child, teacher, and par-

ents. Depending on the child, these goals ranged from just one selected from the Characteristics of a Successful Learner list (i.e., *Focus*, needfully chosen by one immature and squirrely boy) to a
reasonably competent girl choosing three academic goals: (i.e.,
Reading, "do more Independent Reading"; *Writing*, "always make
sure I have a topic at Writing Workshop"; and *Science*, "get to like it
more"). Once these goals were articulated, I then had some guidance
for the specifics to record when doing observations. (Always before I
could never decide *what* precisely to pay attention to when "kid-
watching.")

In December, we mailed home our pilot report cards. They took
as long to complete, if not longer, as any other report card, but now it
was time well spent. The decisions we had to make actually related
to what was heppening in our classrooms. Commentary focused on
(1) explaining and supporting the ratings given on the performance
scales, (2) detailing strengths perceived in the classroom, and (3) describing progress so far on achieving the goals set in October. Most
parents felt they'd been better informed than ever before by a report
card, but some expressed misgivings at not receiving any comparative data. In the second trimester, Student-Led Conferences were
again held, and they went wonderfully. (Afterwards, the boy who'd
chosen "Focus" as his only goal wrote, "It was a dream come true.")
In June, we'll send home another report card like the December one.

What've I learned? Actually, all report cards *should* be burned—
they cannot replace what is better communicated to parents when
they visit their child's classroom and participate in both student-led
conferences as well as three-way conferences. But, the political and
logistical reality of public schools requires, in addition, some kind of
paper form, a report card. Since we're also in the midst of attempting
to get our pilot card adopted by all the 4th- and 5th-grade teachers in
our district, I've also learned that most teachers loathe writing. They
don't mind rating kids on developmental performance scales, are reasonably comfortable with discarding summative grades, but blanch at
a report card form containing one whole blank page that suggests it
should be filled with pertinent written commentary! In order to get our
card accepted, we had to decrease the size of the comment portion.
Oh well, it's still progress and definitely better than anything we've
ever had before. Long ago, John Prine advised in one of his songs to
"blow up the TV, move to the country and feed the kids on peaches."
I realize we can't really burn all report cards, but we must continue to
struggle, discovering ways to more accurately and humanely communicate student progress to parents.

External Assessments: Reflections and Projections

An effective external assessment both reflects and projects: It reflects current practices of exemplary teachers, based on teacher-designed frameworks and current research, and projects models for instruction. The assessment task itself is not a model for instruction, but it provides strategies to be incorporated into the work of the classroom. The assessment is a window through which we can capture vignettes of students in the process of responding, problem solving, interpreting, evaluating, speculating, reflecting—in short, thinking. With an effective scoring and reporting system, teachers can use these vignettes not only to improve instruction but also to provide students and parents with valuable insights into students' achievement, either on a specific task at a particular point in their lives or, in the case of portfolios, on a body of work collected over time.

Schools and districts can use both the on-demand assessment and portfolio assessment as a way of monitoring their success in reaching their instructional goals. Teachers should take the initiative in setting departmental or discipline goals, then decide how to determine the degree to which they are meeting them. Before turning to a discussion of two existing assessment programs, the New Standards Project and the California Learning Record, I will offer two models of assessment that can be implemented at the classroom, school, or district levels: first, an on-demand reading and writing assessment, and second, a portfolio, which might well include an on-demand component.

The On-Demand Assessment

The on-demand test has such a history in our collective memories that the word *test* itself conjures up images of columns of multiple-choice questions, each with several possible right answers. That singular image has gradually given way to other scenarios, most commonly to a writing assessment in which students are allotted from twenty minutes to an hour to write to a given prompt. Writing tests are usually scored holistically, most often, although not always, by teachers trained to apply specific scoring guides to student papers.

Since the early 90s, many school districts, as well as a few states, have initiated large-scale portfolio assessment systems. One useful component of a large-scale portfolio system is an on-demand integrated reading and writing assessment such as the ones piloted by California and by the New Standards Project. Following is an example of an integrated assessment modeled on the prototype developed by the California English language arts assessment development team, a group of teachers who worked over a period of ten years designing and implementing first, a type-specific writing assessment, then an integrated reading and writing assessment. In a large-scale testing situation, the prompt or task should be preceded by a letter to the student telling the purpose of the test, the time frame, and the criteria for scoring. The prototype for the letter and prompt are included in Appendix Five.

Sample Integrated Reading and Writing Prompt
appropriate for staff development workshops

Note: The test format includes full pages for writing or drawing in response to each question or activity.

Section One
Reading

Before You Read

You are going to read the essay "On Going Home" from Joan Didion's 1968 collection *Slouching Toward Bethlehem.* As you read, you may underline parts that you find interesting, have questions about, or think are important. You may write questions and notations in the margin. Remember that while it is not necessary for you to write margin notes as you read, any notes that you do make will become part of the total picture of how you read.

Reading Selection

Text   Margin Notes

After You Have Read

1. What images, thoughts, or feelings came to your mind as you read this essay? Take a few minutes to cluster, list, write, or draw them.
2. What in the text elicited these thoughts and feelings? What in your own experience?

3. Joan Didion writes about going "home." In Column One of the double-entry journal (shown), copy or summarize short passages from the essay that carry the essence of the concept *home* for Joan Didion. In Column Two, explain your choices.

Column One: Passage from the essay	Column Two: Response to the passage
Full page chart for double-entry journal	

4. Didion uses not only her thoughts but also the imagined thoughts of her husband as a way of looking at her family's life. How do you think her husband would describe a visit to her family home? Write an interior monologue (pretend you are the husband) reflecting on the visit. You might include your thoughts about different members of the family, the nature of their conversation, Joan Didion's relationship to her family, and anything else that he might be thinking.

5. Choose two of the quotations listed below and tell what they mean to you in the context of the Didion essay.
   a. ". . . when we talk about sale-leasebacks and right-of-way condemnations we are talking in code about the things we like best. . . ." p. 2, paragraph one
   b. "Marriage is the classic betrayal." p. 2, end of paragraph one
   c. "I smooth out the snapshot (of her grandfather) and look into his face, and do and do not see my own." p. 3, first paragraph

6. Imagine that Didion's daughter is now grown and thinking about what home means to her. Basing your remarks on what you know from reading Joan Didion's essay, write your ideas of how her daughter might define the word *home*.

7. Think about the images and ideas that you have had in your mind as you read and thought about this essay. What single image or idea most clearly focuses the meaning of the essay for you now? Sketch or draw that image.

8. Give your drawing a title: _____

9. Explain your drawing as if you were talking with someone who had not read the essay.

10. This is your chance to tell us anything else about your understanding of this essay—any observations, thoughts, feelings, or questions you may not have expressed earlier.

Section Two
Working with Your Group

Guidelines for Working with Your Group

During this part of the test, your group will discuss ideas stemming from Joan Didion's essay "On Going Home" and prepare for the Writing Assessment. It is important that everyone in the group has a chance to share ideas.

Activities and suggestions for your discussion:

1. Begin your discussion by sharing your ideas after reading and responding to Didion's essay. Suggestions for discussion:
   - Talk about your initial thoughts and whether they changed as you worked through the activities.
   - Share your responses to Didion's ideas about marriage.
2. Moving from your ideas about the essay to your own ideas, talk with your group about how each of you would define the word *home*.
   - What do you mean when you say you are "going home"?
   - What stories or anecdotes come to your mind when you think about the meaning of the word *home* for you.
   - How has the concept of *home* changed from your parent's generation to yours?
3. Try creating a series of metaphors for the idea of *home*. For example, you might begin with these questions, taken from the sun-shadow mandala[1]:
   - What kind of animal is *home* most like in my mind?
   - What color is *home*?
   - What plant is *home* most like?
   - What mineral or gem is *home* most like?
   - What element (air, earth, fire, water) is *home* most like?
4. Working as a group, you're going to integrate your ideas about home with those of Didion. Begin by making a large circle. (Butcher paper works well for this activity.) As a group, decide on one symbol that could stand for Didion's idea of *home*. Have one person in the group draw that symbol or image in the center of the circle. Then, around that symbol, each member of the group should sketch two or three symbols, each showing someone's concept of the word *home*.
5. Discuss the symbols in your circle, explaining how each image stands for one of your ideas.

Section Three
Writing

Writing Situation

Imagine that your class is preparing an anthology of articles, stories, and poems about what the idea of *home* is to different age groups and different groups in society. You have read newspaper and magazine articles about the homeless in California. As part of expanding your understanding of the concept of *home,* you have also read Joan Didion's essay "On Going Home" as well as a number of stories and poems about *home.* Robert Frost says,

> Home is the place where, if you have to go there,
> They have to take you in.

T. S. Eliot said, "Home is where one starts from." Didion, in her essay "On Going Home," writes that she sometimes thinks that "those of us who are now in our thirties were born into the last generation to carry the burden of 'home,' to find in family life the source of all tension and drama." In the first two parts of this assessment, you wrote, and thought about, Didion's ideas as well as your own thoughts about what *home* means to you.

Directions for Writing

Write an essay for the class anthology reflecting on the various meanings of the word *home.* Relate your own ideas about *home* to Didion's ideas as well as to the thoughts of people you know, to other writers whose work you have read, and to people in general. You may refer to the quotations by Frost and Eliot; the important thing is to explore your ideas as thoughtfully and fully as possible.

Scoring the Integrated Reading and Writing Assessment

Scoring papers in a school or district provides one of the best ways to conduct inservice about reading and writing strategies. It is crucial that the school or district provide released time and/or weekend or summer stipends for this work. In addition to the immediate results of student scores, the process for teachers is instructive and collegial, leading to increased collaboration among teachers and greater understanding of how to reach accord on curriculum and pedagogical matters. The best assessment programs combine teach-

er scoring sessions with short staff development workshops, allowing teachers to begin to apply what they have learned before they
ever leave the scoring site.

There are several ways to approach the scoring of this kind of
test. One is to score the reading section (Section One) and the writing section (Section Three) completely separately. In this case, you
would be able to use the Reading Rubric see discussion in Chapter
Two) and the writing rubric for Reflection (see Appendix Three).
Before the scoring of papers, the chief reader and table leaders
should conduct a prereading to select *anchor* or *benchmark* papers
for each score point. One complete set, anchor papers scores 6
through 1, becomes the primary set for anchoring the group during
the training of scorers. Additional papers should be selected and
prescored for use in retraining or calibrating the group during the
reading. For the actual or *live* scoring, there should be a chief reader, table leaders, and readers. Readers should be grouped at tables of
from four to six scorers. In a school or district-wide scoring session,
it is advisable to have separate scoring sessions for reading and
writing. Each paper should be read twice: Assuming that you would
be using the 6-point scale, you would have all discrepant papers
(those with a spread of more than two points) read for the third time
and rescored by the chief reader.

While it is not within the province of this book to offer complete guidelines to the scoring and reporting process, it is important
to emphasize the value of involving teachers in the development
and implementation of assessments at all levels. Classroom teachers
remain the ultimate professional authorities on student performance; to involve them in large-scale assessments helps preserve
the integrity of a unified approach to curriculum and assessment.

A Word about Constructing Rubrics

Rubrics are basic to the entire assessment process, whether it is
classroom assessment or the more formal arena of large-scale testing. Constructing rubrics for the scoring of writing requires some
hard definitions: Are you going to score writing as writing, attending only to those features that transcend rhetorical purpose? Or are
you going to assess specific kinds of writing, as outlined in Chapter
Three? We all acknowledge that if there is anything most English
teachers agree that they know how to do, it is to assess writing. Yet,
if we were to give ten randomly selected student papers to ten randomly selected English teachers, we would, in fact, get some wide-

ly divergent evaluations. On the other hand, we also know that when we train groups of teachers to a rubric or scoring guide, we can achieve exceptionally high rates of agreement about the merits of student papers. Without such a rubric, we generally agree only on the superficial aspects of writing, such as mechanics and spelling. In assessing reading, teachers are eager to have a rubric; without it, they tend to assess the writing about reading rather than the process of reading itself. Fortunately, we now have some models on which to draw, whether we use them or design our own.

Some test-makers prefer to construct task-specific rubrics; these would be applied to individual reading and/or writing prompts and would be used in particular instances rather than applied to a number of different prompts. In constructing rubrics, using categories specific to the purpose of the assessment, the top score description should be established first. A very effective way to design rubrics is to have a group of teachers administer a prompt written to generate a particular type of writing. By first reading and sorting student papers loosely into three levels, then concentrating on the top pile, teachers can set up a description of the top score point. Using student papers as anchors, teachers can then describe subsequent levels of achievement for that grade level.

There are two ways to anchor a rubric. If the goal is to design a grade-level specific rubric, you follow the pattern just outlined. In this scenario, you would have a single rubric that could be used at different grade levels by anchoring it to each grade level. A grade-seven rubric would, in this case, look like the grade ten, but a different set of papers would be used as anchors. The top score for each grade would be, say, a 6 on a scale of 6 to 1.

A different way of setting up the rubric uses standards rather than grade-level anchors. If you want to set up a rubric by which to measure both achievement and growth, using a standards rubric establishes the ideal as the top score or score point 6, in this case. A senior would be expected to be measured against this standard, for example, for graduation. Even a very able seventh grader, however, measured against the same standard, would be expected to place lower on the scale, perhaps at a 4 or 5 level. This kind of rubric would be appropriate as one measure toward an exit-level achievement.

In both cases, the same rubric may be used to score papers at any grade level; it is the purpose of the rubric that is different. For use within individual classrooms, it is most appropriate to use the grade-level concept of rubric for day-to-day teaching.

Large-Scale Portfolio Assessment

A great mountain of material exists on the subject of portfolios, and rightly so. Portfolio use as a classroom learning tool, like the one described in Chapter Five, has burgeoned. Portfolios as instruments of external assessment have been studied, fieldtested, designed, implemented, discarded, redesigned, and reimplemented. There are newsletters providing support to teachers who are beginning to use portfolios. There are state and national assessment projects implementing wide-scale portfolio assessments.

The portfolio concept itself is, of course, not new. Nor was it new in the '90s when the portfolio took off as a major assessment instrument. Artists, from whom we borrowed the term, have been using it for years. In my own teaching notes, I found my earliest use of the term in 1966, when I instituted the portfolio as a culminating activity for, first, a poetry writing class, and, later, all my classes. It makes sense. It works. But the question that keeps arising is, what is the "it" that we mean when we talk about the portfolio as an instrument of assessment? Some of the questions are

- What goes into the portfolio?
- To what extent are the selections prescribed?
- How do we account for individuality if the contents are prescribed?
- If we do not prescribe what goes into the portfolio, how can we grade it so that grades will mean something from one student to another?
- Is the previous question even important?
- Who reads and scores the portfolio?
- What relevance does an externally mandated portfolio have to the classroom curriculum?
- Should an externally mandated portfolio grade "count" in the classroom?
- To what extent would an externally mandated portfolio determine the curriculum of the classes required to submit portfolios?
- Can a classroom portfolio as described in Chapter Five be used for a large-scale assessment? If so, how?

And so on. The questions seem endless, yet we persist in thinking that the portfolio remains the most positive response to teacher and student need for a completely curriculum-integrated assessment. These questions are, of course, being answered by different groups in different ways. The most commonly used design for large-scale portfolios is that which calls for predetermined categories, each with a great deal of latitude as to how the student will fulfill the specified requirements. Most designs also allow for two or three "wild cards" or entries of the student's own choosing.

By far the most important part of the entire portfolio assessment is the student involvement in the process of putting together the portfolio. Nearly all designs call not only for specific kinds of entries but also for student reflections about the pieces in the portfolio. Some call for an introduction, some for a final reflective piece, some for individual reflective pieces about each entry. A few call for student reflective pieces at all of these points. The portfolio, then, emerges as the strongest statement of student self-assessment of any instrument yet designed.

The value of this reflectiveness is another matter. It depends on how the student has been taught to view his or her work. Students who are habitually expected to make judgments about their own work, who are used to sharing works-in-progress with response groups, who work in teams and evaluate their own and their team members' contributions, who know their judgments are taken seriously by their teachers—these are students whose portfolios will reflect confidence, self-worth, and pride in their achievement. They will be able to see their growth over a period of time, see where their strengths are, and see where they need to focus in the next stage of their development as readers and writers. In a large-scale portfolio assessment, these students will excel. These students will receive no surprises when their portfolios are scored by outside evaluators (hopefully teachers) because they will, themselves, already have measured their work against the standards for achievment that have been set, whether these are local, state, or national standards. Can we ask any more from an assessment?

Scoring Portfolios: Dimensions of Learning

Although a number of ways of assessing portfolios have been tried, one working draft that a number of teachers have used successfully at classroom, school, and district levels is that designed by the Educational Testing Service for a proposed statewide portfolio assessment system in California (CLAS). A group of teachers working under the leadership of Bill Thomas, former teacher and administrator, designed a deceptively simple yet elegant system for accommodating many of the questions raised earlier in this chapter. In this system, there is no formula for what is to be included in the portfolio, making it possible for teachers to keep a classroom portfolio that suits the needs of their students and to submit the same portfolio for external assessment purposes. The following material explains the design, the assumptions, and the rubrics, and provides a sample teacher/scorer check list using the rubrics. In this model, it is assumed that classroom teachers would score their own students' portfolios; then a certain percentage of the folders would be sent to the next level—school or district. In the case of statewide assessment, the process would simply move along, with samples being scored by teachers representing districts or areas of the state. By cross-scoring sample portfolios, teachers would receive feedback as to the validity of their local scoring.

Organic Portfolio Assessment

DIMENSIONS OF LEARNING IN LANGUAGE ARTS

The CLAS organic portfolio assessment in language arts is designed to give students opportunities to demonstrate the breadth and depth of their abilities to read, write, listen and speak, as they construct meaning about their lives and the world in which they live. With their teachers' assistance, they select work and other evidence that shows their accomplishment in the following dimensions of learning. The accompanying questions may help teachers and students determine whether the assessment portfolio provides evidence of the dimensions.

CONSTRUCTING MEANING: Students respond to, interpret, analyze, and make connections within and among works of literature and other texts, oral communication, and personal experiences. Students consider multiple perspectives about issues, customs, values, ethics, and beliefs, which they encounter in a variety of texts and personal experiences. They take risks by questioning and evaluating text and oral communication, by making and supporting predictions and inferences, and by developing and defending positions and interpretations. They consider the effect of language, including literal and figurative meaning, connotation and denotation. They reflect on and refine responses, interpretations and analyses by careful revisiting of text and by listening to others.

What in the assessment portfolio shows whether and how well the student:

- responds to what was read or heard with own ideas, interpretations, analyses?
- connects ideas from readings, oral communication, and experiences?

- considers various personal and cultural perspectives?
- takes risks by questioning, by going beyond literal meaning and by developing and defending or explaining a position or point of view?
- considers the effect of language?
- reflects on and refines responses, interpretations and analyses?

COMPOSING AND EXPRESSING IDEAS: Students communicate for a variety of purposes, with a variety of audiences, and in a variety of forms. Their written and oral communication is clearly focused; ideas are coherent, and effectively organized and developed. They use language effectively to compose and express thoughts. They draw on various resources including people, print and non-print materials, technology and self evaluation to help them develop, revise and present written and oral communication. They engage in processes, from planning to publishing and presenting; when appropriate, they do substantial and thoughtful revision leading to polished products. Through editing, they show command of sentence structure and conventions appropriate to audience and purpose.

What in the assessment portfolio shows whether and how well the student:

- communicates for a variety of purposes and audiences and in different genres, both orally and in writing?
- establishes clear focus, coherence, organization and development in communications?
- uses effective language that is appropriate to audience and purpose?
- uses resources to develop, revise and present written and oral communication?
- uses a range of processes from planning to revising, editing and presenting?

Organic Portfolio Assessment Guide—Language Arts

Dimension: Constructing Meaning

CONSTRUCTING MEANING: Students *respond to, interpret, analyze, and make connections* within and among works of literature and other texts, oral communication, and personal experiences. Students *consider multiple perspectives* about issues, customs, values, ethics, and beliefs, which they encounter in a variety of texts and personal experiences. They *take risks* by questioning and evaluating text and oral communication, by making and supporting predictions and inferences, and by developing and defending positions and interpretations. They *consider the effect of language,* including literal and figurative meaning, connotation and denotation. They *reflect on and refine responses, interpretations, and analyses* by careful revisiting of text, by listening to others, and by using a range of resources.

EXEMPLARY	ACCOMPLISHED	DEVELOPING	BEGINNING
RESPONSE, INTERPRETATION, ANALYSIS: explores ideas, issues, relationships and themes by using details from sources to test theories and interpretations	responds, interprets and analyzes by explaining ideas, relationships and themes using references to sources	describes events, people and places with some supporting details from the source	responds by retelling or graphically showing events or facts
CONNECTIONS: uses personal and analytic connections to explore and reflect on ideas and interpretations	explains personal connections to sources or analytic connections between and within sources	makes connections to sources, either personal or analytic	makes personal connections or identifies connections within or between sources in a limited way
PERSPECTIVES: compares and contrasts multiple perspectives in discussing literature, experiences and points of view of others	demonstrates awareness of multiple perspectives in discussing literature, experiences and points of view of others	states or briefly includes more than one perspective in discussing literature, experiences and points of view of others	discusses literature, experiences and points of view of others in terms of own experience
RISKS: questions and evaluates sources, develops and supports student's own interpretations and predictions	takes risks by questioning sources and presenting innovative interpretations and predictions	takes some risks by occasionally questioning sources, or stating interpretations and predictions	responds to sources at factual or literal level
EFFECT OF LANGUAGE: explores effects of literal and figurative language on meaning and presentation, often using specific examples	discusses language effects on meaning and presentation, sometimes using specific examples	identifies the effect of language with some use of examples	focuses on simple aspects of language effect
REFLECTION AND REFINEMENT OF IDEAS: synthesizes information to reflect on and refine responses, interpretations, and analyses; considers several viewpoints and revisits the source	reflects on and refines responses, interpretations, and analyses by revisiting the text or listening to others	makes superficial changes in responses with little evidence of rethinking or refinement	includes little or no evidence of refinement of initial response

Organic Portfolio Assessment Guide—Language Arts

Dimension: Composing and Expressing Ideas

COMPOSING AND EXPRESSING IDEAS: Students communicate for a *variety of purposes*, with a *variety of audiences*, and in a *variety of forms*. Their written and oral communication is clearly *focused*; ideas are *coherent*, and effectively *organized and developed*. They *use language effectively* to compose and express thoughts. They *draw on various resources* including people, print and non-print materials, technology and self-evaluation to help them develop, revise and present written and oral communication. They *engage in processes*, from planning to publishing and presenting; when appropriate they *do substantial and thoughtful revision* leading to polished products. Through *editing*, they show command of sentence structure and conventions appropriate to audience and purpose.

EXEMPLARY	ACCOMPLISHED	DEVELOPING	BEGINNING
AUDIENCES, PURPOSES, GENRES AND STYLES: communicates effectively in an appropriate and personal style to diverse audiences, for varied purposes, using various genres	communicates with an appropriate style to a variety of audiences, for a variety of purposes, using a variety of genres	communicates some awareness of various audiences and purposes; sometimes uses variety in genres	communicates almost exclusively to one audience, usually in the same style and genre
ORGANIZATION AND DEVELOPMENT: demonstrates coherent organization and strong development to communicate ideas clearly and convincingly	demonstrates clear organization; uses details effectively to clarify ideas and arguments	demonstrates organization that is sketchy and sometimes difficult to follow; expresses ideas and arguments using limited details	demonstrates confusing organization or limited development; expresses ideas and arguments with few if any details
LANGUAGE USE: effectively uses persuasive and figurative language and lively description	uses some persuasive, figurative or descriptive language	uses language in a literal way with little creativity	uses language that is sometimes vague, limited, imprecise or repetitive
RESOURCES: uses multiple resources to build and present strong written and oral communication; credits sources appropriately	uses resources to develop, clarify and revise ideas and edit work; attempts to credit sources	uses resources in a limited way to develop ideas and revise or edit work	uses resources sparingly, if at all
REVISING AND EDITING: presents well crafted products that demonstrate clear command of sentence structure and conventions and show evidence of perseverance in revising and editing	presents polished products that demonstrate command of sentence structure and conventions, and reflect revision of ideas and editing of work	presents products that show some command of sentence structure and conventions and some attempts to revise ideas and edit work	presents products with little if any command of sentence structure and conventions; demonstrates few attempts to revise ideas or edit work

Organic Portfolio Assessment

Summary of Student Accomplishment in Language Arts

DIMENSION	Level of performance based on assessment portfolio				
	Beginning	Developing	Accomplished	Exemplary	Not enough evidence
CONSTRUCTING MEANING • responds to, interprets and analyzes sources • makes connections • considers multiple perspectives • takes risks • analyzes language • reflects on performances • revises performances	Rationale:				
COMPOSING AND EXPRESSING • addresses various audiences and purposes • communicates for a variety of purposes and audiences and in different genres • organizes and develops ideas and arguments • uses language effectively • uses resources • revises performances • edits for conventions and style	Rationale:				
SPECIAL ACCOMPLISHMENT Regardless of level of performance on dimensions, student deserves recognition for having: • demonstrated notable growth in one or more areas of language arts, or • through exceptional effort, completed a project, or developed an area of interest or expertise that, for this student, was a major accomplishment	Description:		TO INDICATE, CHECK BOX AND DESCRIBE. ☐		

For classroom teacher use
Complete and include with each assessment portfolio

The Influence of the Public
on Large-Scale Assessment

The power of an externally mandated assessment to affect curriculum and pedagogy is a given. How an assessment affects teaching and learning, however, is dependent on the nature of the instrument and teacher and administrator attitude toward it. On one hand, everyone hopes that test scores will be used to improve instruction; this goal has been achieved only when the assessment system is aligned with a sound curriculum. There are other factors at work surrounding any external assessment: Public opinion about schools is heavily dependent on state test scores; some states have even tied school funding to improvement of scores on state-administered tests. When state-mandated test scores are released for individual students rather than just for school and district comparability, the tests become items of intense public scrutiny. Schools and teachers are likely to be judged by how well their students perform, regardless of the makeup of the school or class population.

Public assessment instruments have become heavily politicized. There are many examples of public controversy surrounding tests, but one has emerged as an example of the potential that assessment has for politicizing education. In the early '90s, the California Learning Assessment System (CLAS) implemented an integrated reading-writing assessment that had been designed by classroom teachers, widely fieldtested, and successfully scored by teachers using teacher-designed rubrics. While it was not a perfect assessment instrument, it was carefully designed to reflect the state framework; as such, it was based on the belief that reading and writing are transactive, purposeful activities. When, in the second year of its implementation, having already been administered to about a million students for the second year, some segments of the population got wind of the fact that the test used works of literature by such notables as Alice Walker and Annie Dillard, the test came tumbling down. Attacks on the literature (the stories allegedly did not promote family values) quickly became submerged under a larger attack: The test asked students to bring their own experience to bear on their interpretations. Students were invited to annotate the text by recording their thoughts and feelings about the literature. Various groups (some from out of state) filed lawsuits against districts for administering a test that "invaded family privacy." Although the legality of the test was upheld in court, it was already too late. Daily newspaper articles fueled what became a political battle involving elections for legislators and the office of governor as well as the state superintendent of schools. The authentic assessment battle was lost, at least for a time. The governor cut all funding for the test and announced that the next assessment would be created and scored by publishers rather than teachers.

I relate this story to illustrate the political stakes tied to external assessment, especially if they involve, as most state assessments do by now, individual scores. I relate it also to urge teachers to become involved in local assessment practice so that they can be knowledgeable about the ramifications of testing programs. Until assessment becomes fully aligned with what goes on in the classroom, it will be a detrimental force in our society, resulting in unfair evaluations of students and teachers, and in class time devoted to teaching to a test that does not reflect the current practices supported by the profession.

On the other hand, there are very positive trends simultaneously at work across the country. Teachers need to know how and where authentic assessment procedures are being practiced, both locally and statewide. With at least some segments of the population supporting reform in assessment as well as in curriculum and school structure, it is critical that teachers take the initiative in designing and implementing school and district assessment programs. Teachers who have been actively involved at the local level are in a prime position to become leaders in affecting the direction of state assessment. Fortunately, we are not working in a vacuum. The National Council of Teachers of English and the International Reading Association have collaborated to produce standards for the profession that may guide teachers in designing compatible assignments and assessments. A number of states have initiated statewide systems that involve performance assessments, chiefly in writing but some branching out to include reading, speaking, and listening. Few states have involved classroom teachers to the degree that would result in a highly integrated teaching/learning/assessment system. The political downfall of CLAS was a severe blow to all teachers nationwide, because this assessment system had set a precedent in involving scores of teachers on its development and implementation team and literally thousands in the scoring sessions. Separate from the work done by individual states, however, there are two exemplary programs that all teachers should know about: one, the New Standards Project, operating on a national level, and the other, the California Learning Record, being piloted on a smaller scale.

The Influence of a Large-Scale On-Demand Assessment on Schools

Can large-scale testing make a difference in our classrooms? Absolutely. Until performance assessment began to infiltrate the testing systems that had controlled the field, the impact of large-scale testing on schools had been either neutral (teachers by and large ignoring the results) or negative (administrators demanding or teachers feeling it important that class time be given to teaching to the test). I say *negative* only because most of the tests have had so little to do with what students should be learning. That's a biased remark, of course, but this is a biased book in favor of a constructivist theory of reading and a process theory of writing.

There are glimmers, however, of a new order. At Twin Hills Middle School in a small town in Sonoma County, California, teachers responded to low scores the first year of the CLAS test by implementing a schoolwide plan that emphasizes writing-to-learn in all subjects. Using the framework of the assessment—reading by active transactions with text and writing for carefully delineated purposes—teachers went to work. They conducted strategy workshops, designed projects involving problem solution, developed cross-curricular units, and generally emphasized student involvement in the processes of writing throughout the day. Teachers divided up the writing types by discipline, each taking the responsibility for teaching, not just assigning specific kinds of writing. Results? Yes. The second year of the CLAS test, and the last, as I described earlier, students at Twin Hills raised their scores dramatically. On the 6-point scale, the first year, their students had only 35% scoring 4 or above. The second year, this figure rose to an astonishing 91%. Scores in the math test rose as well, showing the value of writing in problem solving. The impetus was the CLAS test. The motivators were the teachers. The beneficiaries were the students. While this school undoubtedly will continue its program, other schools, slower to act, will no longer have the stimulus of a model assessment to guide it. The Twin Hills students and the El Sausal students described in Chapter Five have received a great boost in their education, thanks to the teachers who acted on new knowledge to improve their teaching.

The New Standards Assessment System

With the success of these two schools in mind, it is appropriate to turn to a national project that may be able to provide the stimulus for teachers across the country to follow suit. The primary goal of

New Standards[2] is to create an assessment system based on world-class standards of student performance. Centered in the work of Lauren Resnick and her associates at the Learning Research and Development Center of the University of Pittsburgh, with their work supported by the National Center on Education and the Economy, this ambitious project involves nearly a third of the states in the country as "partners" in this venture. The proposed assessment system would consist of three main components, sometimes referred to as the 3 P's—timed *performance* examinations, student *projects* (group and individual), and *portfolios* of student work. Clearly centered in current research and promoting what Resnick calls the "thinking curriculum," this project has the potential for setting standards and model assessment systems that states could adopt to ensure a broad uniformity of approach while preserving multiple opportunities for students to demonstrate their particular abilities. By placing the performance or what may be called the *reference examination*—an on-demand test—within the larger scope of portfolios, this plan preserves the need for comparability from school to school, district to district, and even state to state. New Standards has involved teachers in test design, rubric design, and task development since its beginning; it also involves large groups of teachers in scoring at the cross-state field trials. By honoring the expertise of classroom teachers, New Standards will preserve the two most basic criteria for any successful large-scale testing program: to align the standards and tasks with the most effective curriculum, and to have the classroom teacher ultimately responsible for the major part of the scoring. Using rubrics developed by teachers for the project, classroom teachers can score their own students' projects and portfolios; some teachers can participate in the scoring of the performance or reference tests as well. This project has infinite possibilities as long as it stays in touch with the heart and mind of the profession.

The California Learning Record

The California learning Record[3] (CLR) yields a portfolio of information about a student's annual academic progress based on student performance of authentic language and literacy tasks and on consultations with parents and the students themselves. Spearheaded by Mary Barr at the Center for Language in Learning, and pilot-tested by California teachers since 1988, the CLR is an adaptation of the *Primary Language Record,* developed at the Centre for Language in Prima-

ry Education for K–6 use in London, England. Major California contributions are to extend the record to middle and secondary schools,
to extend the fields of discipline to all subject areas, including mathematics, and to develop a system of student assessment based on
classroom work samples and observations that can be validated as
accurate and fair for public accountability purposes.

The CLR is built on principles that are designed to prepare students for the complexities of the information ages, with emphases on

- thoughtfulness over rote learning
- performance over deficit
- individual development meshed with grade-level expectations
- the strengths of being bilingual and of understanding cultures
  beyond one's own

In classrooms where these principles guide students, classroom
assessment of student achievement must value growth and development over time. Forms of assessment must be appropriate to the individual and to the subject matter under study. To this end, many
teachers are turning to the use of portfolios of student work. They
and, increasingly, their students can then select, from classroom
portfolios, samples for large-scale assessment purposes.

Integral to the CLR are five dimensions of learning, which serve
as a framework through which to view student learning. Teachers
evaluate student progress along continua of these five dimensions
as students reveal what and how they are learning in oral classroom
tasks as well as through their reading and their writing:

- confidence and independence
- experience
- skills and strategies
- knowledge and understanding
- ability to reflect

The CLR is available in handbook form, complete with instructions and forms for application. There is a strong support system of
core development teachers who have pioneered the program and
serve as coaches to other teachers who are interested in first-hand
knowledge of how to collect data from students and parents as well
as how to become careful observers of their students and collectors
of student work. One of the most compelling features of this program
is the involvement of students and parents in the process. At first
glance, it may seem unwieldy, but teachers who have applied the
system in their classes have learned an essential truth about restruc-

turing: A new system does not mean adding to what you are already doing; it means changing the way you are doing it. For those teachers willing to look at their own values as they plan how to conduct assessment in their classrooms, learning a system such as that offered by the CLR means learning to use time in a different, more effective way.

Epilogue

Measuring Up: An Endnote

Every culture has its tricksters: For the past twenty years, the coyote of our culture has been the multiple-choice test—tricky by design and intent—that has spelled out the future for our students. Recently, the papers heralded reforms in the SAT, acknowledging that the new test would not depend, *as it had before,* on questions intended to trick students into wrong answers. The old test, they went on to admit, encouraged the plethora of cram courses created to teach students how to avoid the pitfalls of deceptive questions.

The direction is clear. The trickster has lost ground. Still, the myths remain strong in some parts of the United States, and in some sections of all parts of this country. The most prevalent myths supporting a testing based on trickery are the following.

Myth 1: The Myth of Objectivity

Heisenberg's principle that the observer affects the observed changed the nature of the scientific view of objectivity; it has been slower in reaching educational views of testing. This myth fails to acknowledge that all test items, including those purportedly *objective,* are, in a sense, subjective: Correct answers always lie in the minds of the test-makers. We must design tests that encourage students to make meaning from interactions: student–text–context. Math, science, history/social studies, English—all of these disciplines are currently fieldtesting interactive performance assessments. Many of them are under attack from those who believe this myth.

Myth 2: The Myth of Learning as an Isolated Activity

A study conducted with orphaned infants in Central America showed that babies raised so that they could see and hear people on television but who had little interaction with human beings did not learn to speak. The development of language requires communication. We must teach students to be aware of how their own past experiences—with texts, with people, with events, with self—affect the meaning that they make as they read and write. We must create schools that encourage students to work collaboratively on projects. Our society depends on our working together.

Myth 3: The Myth That All People Learn in Identical Ways

It seems simplistic now even to include this myth, but our testing system is built on an outmoded view of how people learn. Beginning in the '70s, with the first popular reports of brain research, and continuing into the '90s, with Howard Gardner's work on multiple intelligences, we now have the knowledge to design assessments that are appropriate for all learners. We must provide options to involve students in multiple ways to read the texts of their world: We must provide opportunities for them to work with the four functions—observation, analysis, imagination, and feelings. Assessment itself should be part of everyday learning, with continual opportunities for informed self-evaluation.

We need to provide multiple opportunities for assessment using different learning modalities. One of the dangers of this myth is that it leads to formulaic teaching, formulaic learning, and formulaic assessment. The five-paragraph essay, for example, is a perfectly legitimate form for an essay. When it becomes a formula for writing every kind of essay, however, it becomes a mind-limiting strategy that stifles naturally evolving thought processes. It gives students a false sense of security. There is no single pattern that will enable students to use their own minds in reading a piece of literature, solving a mathematical problem, or writing up an experiment in science.

Teachers are the first to acknowledge that they need more help in improving the quality of their teaching. They need more books, more materials, better external assessments. Teachers need to connect with researchers; they need to become researchers themselves. They need time to develop new strategies. Perhaps even more critically than any of these needs, however, is that they need time to talk and work with each other. Making meaning is not something that teachers expect only of their students; they expect it of themselves. Until teachers make meaning for themselves—of how to develop and use standards, of how to translate current theories about reading into their teaching, of how to make sense of technological resources, of how to implement the new theories underlying authentic assessment—they will be unable to improve the quality of their teaching.

What are the kinds of outcomes that ensue from the shift from multiple-choice testing to authentic, performance assessment? Here are a few items, just for starters:

	From multiple-choice testing	**From performance-based assessment**
Reading	• Students employ lower-level thinking skills: simple recall of facts. • Students learn to discriminate among interpretations others have made.	• Students engage interactively with the text. • Students use their own prior knowledge as they make meaning from text. • Students employ higher-level thinking processes such as deferred judgment, multiple interpretations, analysis, evaluation.
Writing	• Students discriminate among various pre-written versions of a text to determine the version most nearly approaching standard written English. • Students learn to edit others' work: punctuate, select standard English forms of usage, agreement, verb forms, spelling, etc.	• Students wrestle with the processes involved in composing an essay, story, or poem. • Students respond to the specific requirements of a prompt and employ suitable strategies for a particular purpose. • Students acknowledge the needs of an identified audience, shaping their work directly to the constraints of the situation.

Teacher Involvement Is the Mind and the Heart of Authentic Assessment

Teachers and administrators need

- to be informed
  - about curriculum options
  - about theories of learning, of reading, of writing
  - about teaching strategies that are based on current learning theories
  - about performance-based, authentic assessment
- to take a leadership role
  - in continuing staff development to address the implications of authentic assessment
  - for broadening instructional strategies for all students
  - for selecting vital and appropriate textbooks and teaching materials
  - for improving both classroom and grade-level assessments, incorporating portfolio assessment
  - for including in the portfolios ways of documenting growth and achievement in all forms of literacy and in varied ways of expressing meaning—including graphics, drama, film, etc.

Above all, teachers need to support each other in professional involvement, understanding that a good teacher is not necessarily one who is in the classroom every day of the week. Teachers need to observe and coach each other, trade classrooms, and train substitutes to carry on the student-centered work of the class so that teachers can spend work time improving their ability to teach. With such cooperation, assessment will go far beyond the limitations of the multiple-choice test and open up possibilities of using assessment to improve what we are all about—enabling our children to value and make meaning of literature, of experience, of talking with others, of school, of their own lives.

During the past ten years, teachers learned *what* works. During the next ten, we will focus on *why*. With the internalization of learning modes and teaching strategies we know are successful—and an increasingly sophisticated ability to articulate why these practices work—we will be able to move with confidence and conviction into the political arena to influence legislation, to construct assessment programs that will—we know—be used to assess not only our students, but also us, as teachers. We will be willing to be held accountable when certain criteria are met:

- when we—and our students—are measured by the standards *we set*
- when we are the test-makers and we test what we teach—the way we teach it—for reasons we can articulate to students, parents, administrators, legislators, and business leaders.

It is not enough to say, "It works." We must be able to explain and document our knowledge.

Assessment Directions

In the next ten years, I hope we will see a revolution in assessment. It has already begun, but it has a long way to go. What I hope to see—in ten years, or before—is an assessment program that will address these concerns:

1. A three-tiered program:
   a. Classroom assessment: an individual assessment program involving teacher, student, and family
   b. A school/district assessment: an individual assessment program for the purposes of program evaluation as well as individual reporting and guidance; primary goal is in curriculum evaluation and development of strategies to implement goals
   c. Large-scale assessment: an assessment program that looks at trends, comparative data; this program would not assign individual scores, but would use matrix sampling to assess a wide range of reading and writing tasks
2. An integrated assessment of an integrated curriculum: one that recognizes the intertextuality of reading and writing (the similarities *and* the differences) as well as the essential nature of speaking and listening/collaboration and audience
3. The role of purpose elevated to its central position in the assignment and assessment of English language arts activities
4. A program that not only acknowledges but also builds on an understanding of the four functions, enabling students to connect with the texts of their worlds through *observation*; to live through experience by involving the *imagination*; to transact with texts through *analysis* and reflection; and to retain their ability to be compassionate human beings through the educated use of their *feelings*
5. Provision for teacher involvement at all levels of assessment

6. Wide use of alternative performance-based assessment methods
7. Increased understanding and use of self-assessment, certainly in portfolios but, even more importantly, as an ongoing part of everyday teaching and learning. Self-assessment is the most valid measure we have of whether a writer has achieved his or her purpose. Far from being an ability with which we are born, fully formed like Athena springing from the head of Zeus, self-assessment is an art that must be taught, nurtured, given an opportunity to grow, then accepted and honored. It is a complex spiral path we as teachers must take as we first create an environment in which self-assessment is a natural, ongoing part of every aspect of the curriculum, and then provide the scaffolding on which students can evaluate their growth and their achievement in a way that has meaning outside themselves, outside the classroom. Ultimately, our students must go into the world of work with an accurate picture of how they best fit into the larger community.

Assessment as Appreciation

We receive so many gifts. How do we evaluate the gifts that our students give us? We evaluate them by looking at the root word within evaluation: *value*. Every time we acknowledge that we value a student's achievement, effort, growth, we are measuring success. By becoming more mindful observers of our students, we can find more ways to acknowledge the successes that don't fall into the traditional categories of learning.

The fact that you are reading these words attests to the power of the writing/teaching community. Every day you go into your classroom where you find your own unique mix of human beings; you find your own special problems and special promises. There, in your classroom, you can assess what you are doing, join the teacher/researchers already hard at work across the United States, and learn from your students, from professional journals, from your colleagues, from your own struggles and successes.

My hope is that your students, like Mirna Lau, a fifteen-year-old student who wrote this poem after being in the United States scarcely a year, will write with joy and confidence, whatever the level of their current involvement with the language.

Dedicated to the Alameda High School Teachers

Even though, my dearly loving teachers,
your time is as precious as all
the richest jewelry in the world,
it never would lose its valuable
signification of gold.

Always, you will fight a battle in
your country with a book in your hands
to defeat a war of ignorance
and will fill up with richness
knowledge of our Mother's Earth.

Afterwards, you are devoting your lives
without getting any medal of honor,
but in your consciences will remain
your lovely dedication to the students
with the placidity of tenderness.

—Mirna Lau

Appendix One

The Sun-Shadow Mandala

The sun-shadow mandala involves students in working with dualities found within themselves, others, literary characters, character relationships, or concepts. The process of making a mandala moves from making metaphors (using the functions of *imagine* and *feel*), to choosing specific attributes for each metaphor (using the functions of *observe* and *analyze*), to integrating them into a circular design. The student uses all four functions in the process of planning, drawing the mandala, and weaving both the sun and shadow metaphors into sentences that frame the drawing.

The use of the terms *sun* and *shadow* is consistent with an archetypal approach to metaphor. Students select their sun images by thinking analytically, considering alternatives; they are using the "sun side" or Apollonian aspect of their minds. They select shadow images by moving through a process of word choices, arriving at their images by opposition; they are using the "shadow side" of their minds, more clearly associated with mythology of the moon.

The concept of sun-shadow images arises from considering the place of dualities in literature and in our lives. Although it may seem superficial to think in terms of dualities, our history is filled with philosophies that are built on concepts of opposites. (Charles Hampden-Turner's *Maps of the Mind* is a useful, graphically depicted history of the philosophies of dualities throughout history.) It is important to acknowledge that things are never as simple as good and evil, war and peace, inner and outer, the haves and the have nots. Being aware of dualities, however, is a helpful starting point for understanding the more subtle complexities of personalities and motivations for human behavior.

The making of mandalas, reinforcing as it does the foundations of reading and writing, trains students of all ages to think both visually and symbolically. It teaches and reinforces the concepts of symbol or metaphor, abstraction, and opposition. It leads from visualization and fantasy to drawing to writing, a natural progression. As students move from making metaphors (using the functions of *imagine* and *feel*) to drawing them, integrating language as appropriate (using the functions of *observe, analyze*), they are integrating various aspects of an abstraction into the graphic mandala form.

Students learn the concepts of *simile/metaphor, abstract/concrete,* and *general/specific* as they generate their images. The word search involved in the making of the mandala chart encourages precision of word choice and understanding of synonyms, antonyms, and connotations, all in the context of the student's process of uncovering the shadow images. As students construct their mandala sentences, they play with language, learning to generate sophisticated, grammatically correct sentences while integrating the various elements of their mandalas.

The act of *drawing* the mandala requires the student to show the relationships among the symbols by size, color, placement, and interaction. As students visually integrate these seemingly disparate elements of character, the developing "whole" of their mandala, like Buckminster Fuller's geodesic dome, becomes greater than the sum of its parts. They are able to see connections, to recognize the multiple layers, dimensions, and interrelationships of character, concept, and technique. This new understanding, whether conscious or subliminal, sets up a pattern of thinking that is reflected in the depth and richness of their writing.

In addition to acting as a catalyst for developing visual and metaphorical thinking behaviors, the process of comparing a character or an idea to archetypal symbols (an animal, a plant, an element), drawing the symbols, then posing reasons for their choices leads students to a deeper understanding of personality. As they begin to uncover both sun and shadow traits and to validate these traits by returning to the text, students become aware of nuances in both character and technique. They begin to see the power in what an author chooses *not* to say, and to understand how the *unsaid* as well as the *said* can be used to generate meaning. In becoming aware of these subtle personality traits, students gain insights into both cultural and personal values. This process often leads them quite naturally to compare themselves with the literary or historical characters they are studying; and, as they make these connections, they gain insight into the qualities that connect us all as members of the human community.

For a full discussion of the sun-shadow mandala, with classroom applications and student examples, see *Drawing Your Own Conclusions: Graphic Strategies for Reading, Writing, and Thinking*, by Fran Claggett and Joan Brown (Heinemann-Boynton/Cook, 1992).

Appendix Two

Some Questions to Ask about Portfolios: Why and How Should We Use Them?

- **What kind of portfolios?**
  English classes only? Writing only? Reading and writing?
  Evidence of projects? Graphics? All disciplines?

- **Who will use the portfolios?**
  Students only? Teachers only? Teachers and students?
  Parents? Administrators?

- **What is the makeup of the portfolios and who decides what goes into them?**

- **Who is to grade the portfolios?**
  The teacher in the individual classroom?
  Groups of teachers within one department?
  Teachers representing all disciplines?
  Teachers who do not know the students or the school? (district level? state level?)

- **How can portfolios be used to effect curricular change?**
  To identify school strengths and needs for improvement?
  To help students and teachers set goals?
  To examine writing in different modes and genres?
  To design a sequence in writing instruction?
  To provide pro tem evaluation?

To foster professionalism and collaboration within and across departments?

To evaluate the kinds of assignments given students?

To encourage writing in all subjects?

- **How are portfolios to be graded?**
  By individual pieces?
  As a whole "lifework" for the term?
  By its reflectiveness?
  By student growth?
  By student achievement?

- **What are we assessing with these portfolios?**
  Student growth?
  Achievement?
  Evidence of collaborative learning?
  Evidence of thinking in all of the four functions (observe, analyze, imagine, feel)?

- **How can we build in reflectiveness, self-evaluation?**
  Introduction to entire portfolio?
  Reflections on each piece included?
  Final reflection on the whole portfolio?

Appendix Three

Reflective Essay Scoring Guide

The reflective essay, characterized by exploration and discovery, is rooted in a specific experience or observation but moves outward from the personal implications of that experience to those of a more general nature.

Characteristics of the Reflective Essay

Inspired by an observation or a personal occasion, the reflective writer makes connections between the stimulus of experience and the ideas it generates. The reflective writer explores these connections in the light of other experiences, often arriving at new dimensions of the original thought. Reflective writing shows a process of thinking as much as a product, achieving for the writer, and often for the reader, a new understanding or insight.

Characteristics of reflective writing, then, include a presentation of the stimulus for writing, which we call the *occasion*, plus the written r*eflection* that explores its meaning for the writer.

Reflective essays are grounded in the concrete. An ordinary thing seen, done, read, overheard, or experienced can trigger the writer to explore what that occasion might say about the self, and, by extension, about the human condition. Occasions for reflection might be observations of a natural phenomenon, an experience with another person or group of persons, a quotation, or perhaps a familiar proverb. The occasion becomes the stimulus for the writer to explore and interpret some aspect of people in general or of the natural world.

Among the types of writing defined by CLAS, the reflective essay is closest to autobiographical incident and observational writing. Although the reflective essay often begins in the careful description of observation or the narration of autobiographical incident, it moves to a different level of abstraction. Reflective writers explore the meaning of the incident or observation not only for themselves, but also for people in general. It is this people-in-general aspect of reflection—exploring the larger social implications of an idea—that is the hallmark of the reflective essay.

The flow of thinking in exploring an idea may take shapes such as the following. The writer may

- present the occasion (narrate a full incident or describe an observation), choosing details and images carefully as a way to ground the reflection that follows. The reflection then moves off on its own, perhaps with some reference to the initiating occasion.
- launch an occasion but then move in and out of it along the way, reflecting on the ideas it suggests
- construct a web of related, often parallel experiences or observations that show, by their interrelatedness, a theme underlying common human experiences
- begin with a quotation, proverb, or general statement and test personal experience against it, reflecting on how each experience relates to the general concept. The reflection becomes refined more fully with each example.

Whatever thought pattern emerges, the writer's reflections explore the meaning of the occasion beyond the personal to the general.

Students who lack experience reading and writing the reflective essay usually respond in limited ways to prompts: (1) They fail to ground their reflections in concrete observations or personal anecdotes or do so only superficially and then write a conventional "expository" essay about the idea in the topic; (2) they narrate a relevant personal experience but then neglect to explore the idea it suggests or do so only briefly, often in a moralizing way; or (3) they write a meditation rather than a reflection, turning an idea over and over but not grounding their ideas in personal experience or observation.

While the *rhetorical* aspect of the assessment focuses on the distinctive features of writing types, the *effectiveness* aspect guides us to look carefully at the more comprehensive features of coherence and style. *Coherence*, a sense of organization, flow, and focus, is essential to all good writing. The coherent essay has a clear direction, each section flowing naturally from the preceding one. Coherence is demonstrated to readers through emphasis, organization, logic, and repetition achieved through recurrences of language, syntax, and ideas. *Style*, for the purposes of this assessment, is observable in two written language features: (1) *sentence control,* and (2) *word choice* or *diction*. In assessment of the effectiveness of style, the primary considerations are *appropriateness, precision,* and *control*.

Score Point 6: Exceptional Achievement

Occasion for reflection. The writer of a 6-point essay presents the occasion for reflection (a thing seen, read, or experienced) richly and memorably, often with the fine detail of the naturalist or autobiographer. Though the occasion does not dominate the essay at the expense of reflection, it is usually presented in extended, concrete detail. Whether an anecdote or an observation of nature or a literary text, the occasion grounds the entire essay in a concrete experience.

The writer of a 6-point paper may use such strategies as these:

- describe an animal, object, or phenomenon, using concrete language rich in sensory detail
- record specific behaviors, properties, or actions, often using narrative strategies such as pacing, dialogue, or action
- cite a quotation or a specific instance as a basis for reflection
- Construct a web of related, often parallel experiences that serve as the combined "occasion"

Reflection. The reflection about the idea suggested by the occasion is exceptionally thoughtful and perceptive. The reflection tends to be extended, reflecting a serious, sometimes tenacious probing and exploring of the subject. There is movement in the essay; it does not become mired down in repetition of ideas without expansion or different angles subtly changing the force of the exploration.

The reflection may include generalization about the subject relevant to the writer's own life, but must include consideration of the larger social implications as well. Most essays scored 6 will have some explicit, insightful general reflection. In some notable papers, however, the writer's presentation of the occasion is couched in such a way that the reader sees that the occasion clearly stands for an entire class of events characteristic of human nature or of social interaction. In these papers the general reflection is implicit, embedded in phrases or clauses that cue the reader to move beyond the specific occasion to the abstraction that underlies it. The tone, established by a distancing of self from occasion, clearly conveys the reflective nature of such essays.

The reflection of a 6 paper often reveals discovery or deepening insight and may end without a sense of conclusiveness about the subject. The paper itself, however, will have an appropriate sense of conclusion.

Coherence and style. The 6 essay has clear coherence, each section flowing naturally from the previous one. Emphasis, organization, and repetition are achieved through recurrences of language, syntax, and ideas. Each section of the essay is developed coherently. Because of the nature of reflection, there may be abrupt shifts of focus, but the careful reader will see that these shifts are warranted by association-al leaps of mind. The effective paper will eventually account for the full range of shifts, however, either explicitly or implicitly.

Language is used consistently with imagination, precision, and appropriateness. The writer exhibits an exceptional control of sentence structures, using a variety of structures as appropriate to the context of the essay.

Score Point 5: Commendable Achievement

Occasion for reflection. Like a 6-point essay, score point 5 presents an extended concrete occasion. The occasion does not dominate the essay at the expense of reflection. A 5 lacks only the vividness and impact of a 6-point essay.

Reflection. The writer engages in extended, thoughtful reflection with at least some general reflection. The occasional 5 essay establishes a reflective tone by an effective distancing of self from the occasion. The 5 paper will not carry it through so conclusively, however. Both personal and general reflection are serious and honest but lack the intellectual leaps and fresh insights of a 6 paper. The 5 essay reaches beyond obvious statements about the occasion and idea. The reflection is not wholly predictable and may include a sense of discovery without the powerful insights of the 6.

Coherence and style. Like the 6 essay, the 5 has clear direction and coherence; it may, however, lack the overall smoothness of the 6-point essay. A 5-point essay will show the writer's ability to use words with precision and appropriateness. Word choice may show less versatility than in the 6 paper; however, the diction is still consistently strong and controlled throughout the essay. The writer exhibits sustained control of sentence structures appropriate to the context.

Score Point 4: Adequate Achievement

Occasion for reflection. The 4-point essay presents a concrete occasion but may lack the detail or specificity of a 5- or 6-point essay. In some papers, a well-developed, elaborated occasion, such as an autobiographical incident, may dominate the essay but not to the point of obscuring the reflective aspects of the paper.

Reflection. Reflection will indicate a serious attempt to explore the idea suggested by the occasion but may be less well grounded in that specific occasion. Some details may seem extraneous, interrupting the purposeful exploratory movement of the essay. The reflection, while it may be extensive, is likely to be predictable or commonplace. The writer may rely on personal reflections about the occasion but will still include at least a brief general reflection. A 4-point essay may be characterized by thoughtfulness rather than by a sense of exploration and discovery.

Coherence and style. The 4-point essay may fall into predictable patterns. It occasionally suffers from lapses in organization. Coherence may be disrupted by abrupt changes in direction that are not accounted for by the nature of the essay.

The language in the 4-point essay may be somewhat conventional and predictable. The essay shows a sustained control of sentence structure but may have less variety than the 5 and 6 papers.

Score Point 3: Some Evidence of Achievement

Occasion for reflection. The writer usually presents an occasion, but it may either be brief or dominate the essay. In a number of papers, what appears at first reading to be *occasions* may actually be examples chosen to illustrate an initial generalization or conclusion.

Reflection. The essay may have a meandering rather than purposefully exploratory quality. Although the reader can understand the major ideas, there may be irrelevant details, digressions, and/or repetitions. The 3-point essay may rely on personal reflection to the exclusion of general reflection. Reflection will seem obvious or even superficial, often taking the form of moralizing.

Some 3-point essays will offer only an extended reflection or meditation about the idea in the prompt, with little grounding in an occasion. The essay may seem generally competent and the medita-tion may be engaging, but the lack of a carefully grounded occasion keeps such papers from receiving higher than a score point 3.

Coherence and style. Although the major ideas in the 3 essay are clear, there may be lapses in coherence caused by irrelevant details, digressions, and/or repetitions.

The writer shows basic control of simple sentences, but the 3-point essay has little sentence variety. Word choice is usually ap-propriate to the content; however, the writer may rely on general rather than specific language.

Score Point 2: Little Evidence of Achievement

Occasion for reflection. The occasion may be brief or it may domi-nate the essay. There may be no occasion or the essay may be all occasion with little or no reflection.

Reflection. If there is an occasion, the reflection may be additive or unfocused. It may be very brief and simplistic, often leaning toward statements of belief or opinion rather than reflection. Some details may be irrelevant. Some 2-point essays may be extended personal or generalized reflections on a topic with only a tangential or no grounding at all in an occasion.

Coherence and style. The 2 essay may lack coherence. Ideas are likely to be undeveloped and disconnected. The writer uses little variety in sentence structure and may have lapses in sentence con-trol. Word choice may be inappropriate.

Score Point 1: Minimal Evidence of Achievement

Occasion for reflection. There may be no occasion. If there is an oc-casion, it will be very brief and devoid of specificity or concrete-ness.

Reflection. There is no reflection. There may be brief and superfi-cial attempts at definition or statements of opinion rather than re-flection.

Coherence and style. The 1-point essay is characterized by a lack of coherence. There may be frequent lapses in sentence sense and word choice.

Appendix Four

Reading Stances and Suggested Questions

(For reading both aesthetically and efferently incorporating reading stances as defined by Judith Langer)

AESTHETIC READING	EFFERENT READING

A. Initial Envisionments

Articulating an initial impression	*Recording an initial understanding*
What does the text mean to you?	What do you now understand about this topic?
What did you think about the text when you finished reading it?	
What do you make of the text?	

B. Developing an Interpretation
(making meaning; negotiating meaning)

Presenting an elaborated interpretation	*Refining your interpretation*
How do things change or remain the same in the text?	What ideas do you take away from the experience of reading this text and where did you get these ideas?
What do you know about _____(some aspect of the text) and how do you know it?	

AESTHETIC READING	EFFERENT READING
How would you answer a question you still have about the text?	What in the text helped clarify your understanding or influenced your opinion?
What do you think about _____ (some value or issue in the text)?	What did you already know that helped you understand this topic?
Why do things happen the way they do in this text?	

C. Reflection/Rethinking

Reflecting on personal experience	*Rethinking what you know*
How did reading this text change or confirm your understanding of human nature?	How does what you learned change what you thought you knew?
What thoughts about your own ideas or attitudes did reading this text stimulate?	How might you use what you learned from reading this text?

D. Demonstrating a Critical Stance

Demonstrating a critical stance	*Demonstrating a critical stance*
How does the way the text is written help shape your interpretation?	How does the way this text is written influence your understanding or opinion?
Do you think this is a good or bad text of its type? Why?	How true or how convincing is this text?
What other texts does this text remind you of?	Was there anything about the way the text was organized that helped you understand it?
How does this text lend itself to alternative interpretations?	What other texts on this topic have you read?
What would you like to say about the form of this text?	What special strategies did you notice the writer using?

AESTHETIC READING

Some people believe this text means_____. Explain why you agree or disagree.

How would you explain what type of text this is?

What was the most meaningful part of the text for you and why?

EFFERENT READING

Do you think the text provided all the information you needed? If not, how could you get more information?

Appendix Five

Prototype Developed for California Integrated Reading and Writing Assessment

Section One: Focus on Reading

1. Getting Ready to Read

The prereading section presents a brief introduction to the assessment task; it includes the title of the text, the author, the historical context (if relevant), and any other information necessary to orient the reader. Students learn whether the text is excerpted. They also learn whether additional texts will be introduced later in the task. A brief statement directs students to read the text and annotate, ask questions, draw, or write responses in the margin.

2. After You Read

All tasks have some version of an initial response question or graphic activity. These questions are designed to elicit students' immediate responses—feelings, questions, opinions, memories, ideas. Several additional questions or activities help students move beyond their initial response to a deeper exploration of meaning.

A final section, "This is your page to tell us . . . ," gives students the opportunity to address any insights, issues, or concerns that developed during the reading process, responses that might not have been elicited by other activities. Students may, through their writing or drawing on this page, come to closure and/or discover new insights emerging from the text and/or from their reading experience.

Section Two: Collaborative Work

Directions provide instructions for students to meet in groups of students who have read the same selections. Activities for this section serve two purposes: to extend students' reading experience and to initiate prewriting activities that they will use in Section Three, the writing assessment.

Section Three: Focus on Writing

The writing prompt has two parts, the *Writing Situation* and *Directions for Writing*.

Writing Situation

This section establishes a framework for the writing prompt and provides students with a context for their writing. It orients students to a type of writing only by posing a plausible situation in which that type of writing would naturally occur. It provides specific background about the topic as well as any material they might need, such as a selection of literature, a photograph, or a chart. The occasion for writing is specified in this section, preparing students to be thinking about their intended readers.

Directions for Writing

The second section gives students the specifics regarding the assignment's topic, intent, potential audience, and any other information students need in order to respond to the prompt.

Appendix Six

End-of-Term Assessment: One Model

At the end of an assessment term, students engage in a process of self-assessment. They have, by this time, learned the value of self-assessment. At the end of a term, students gather together whatever evidence they have of their work—writing folders, notebooks, graphics, reading journals, videotapes. Their first task is to organize their ideas. To help them with this task, they fill out the *Student Self-Assessment Chart* (Figure A6-1). They generally work in small groups, talking about the various papers and projects they have completed, looking over and collecting drafts of papers or evidence of their work on projects. They list all of the papers or projects they can remember. A group memory helps here. I do not provide them with a listing, however, as I am always interested to see how they organize and name aspects of the course. As they fill out the Student Self-Assessment Chart, they organize the evidence of their work.

After they have competed the chart, we discuss the *End-of-Term Portfolio*. Purposes may vary, depending on the class, but generally, we establish such purposes as these:

The portfolio will contain work that

- students wish to keep for themselves
- might be useful for the rest of the course or for future courses
- demonstrates students' best work for the term
- is noteworthy for some more specific reason, such as demonstrating growth in a particular area

In order to make the portfolios useful for assessment, they follow the following format:

End-of-Term Portfolio

Cover: The cover must include name, date, course title and section. For the cover, students may use a graphic already completed or they may choose to design a portfolio cover. It need not be elaborate or artistic; the criterion is that the cover in some way reflect the student's work for the term.

Table of Contents: All work included must be listed as part of the Table of Contents. Pages are are numbered and recorded in the Table of Contents.

Introduction: The self-evaluation essay is the student's introduction to the portfolio.

Papers and Projects: Papers are numbered and organized in whatever way suits the purpose of the student. A separate page is included for each group project and/or graphic that cannot be included in the portfolio; on this page the project or graphic is named and described briefly; the student describes his/her role in the project or graphic.

Student Self-Assessment Chart: The chart is included as the final page of the portfolio. It should be listed in the Table of Contents.

End-of-Term Student Self-Assessment Chart

Fill out the chart by naming or describing papers or projects completed this term. For each item, use the numbers 1 (low) to 5 (high) to indicate the four aspects of your involvement. Following completion of the chart, write the Self–Assessment Essay as described on the next page.

Paper or Project: Brief Description	Level of Interest	Level of Value	Degree of Participation	Quality of Participation

Figure A6-1

Student Self-Assessment Essay

After students have filled out this chart, they write a self-evaluation essay reflecting on their work for the past term and articulating ideas about what they hope to achieve in the next. They refer specifically to papers and projects listed in the chart, elaborating on their assessments of a paper/project's interest or value; commenting on reasons for their lack of involvement, perhaps; explaining why they have assessed the quality of their work as they have.

As a conclusion to the self-assessment essay, students look at the totality of their involvement and work over the term and, in schools where letter grades are part of the reporting system, assign a letter grade to their work for the term. They know that any disparity with the teacher's evaluation, after the teacher has reviewed their charts and read their essays, will lead to a conference. Ideally, the teacher would confer with each student about his or her grade; realistically, given the student load in many high schools, it may not be possible to confer with each student at the end of each grading period. This compromise assumes, of course, that there will have been teacher-student conferences periodically throughout the term.

Suggested Directions to Students:

After you have filled out this chart, write a self-evaluation essay reflecting on your work for the past term and articulating ideas about what you hope to achieve in the next. Refer specifically to papers and projects listed in the chart, elaborating on your assessments of a paper/project's interest or value; commenting on reasons for your lack of involvement, perhaps; explaining why you have assessed the quality of your work as you have.

As a conclusion to the self-assessment essay, look at the totality of your involvement and work over the term and assign a letter grade to your work for the term. You know that we will discuss your grade if I have come to a different evaluation of your work for this term.

Appendix Seven

A Word about Teacher Portfolios

Many teacher education programs now require prospective teachers to prepare portfolios to take with them on job interviews. Practicing teachers, however, are finding that keeping portfolios serves more than providing an edge in interviews. Some teachers have begun using portfolios to keep a running record of their own professional experience, with ongoing entries for teaching strategies, reading responses to professional articles and books, results of their own classroom research studies, successful units, and so on.

We all know students who balk at requirements; the following piece was written not by a student, but by a teacher who balked at an assignment to create a professional portfolio as part of the summer program of the California Literature Project. As you will see, the act of writing out her objections led to unexpected insights not only about the value of portfolios, but also about her own ways of thinking about her life.

Portfolio—An Internal Dialogue

by Barbara Armstrong

A: You seem to be resisting doing this assignment. What have you got against making a portfolio?

B: I'm not really sure, but I ran across a poem of Mary Oliver's yesterday, and it pretty much expresses my feelings on the subject.

The poem's called "Dogfish." Listen to this:

> You don't want to hear the story
> of my life, and anyway
> I don't want to tell it, I want to listen
> to the enormous waterfalls of the sun

A: Hmm. ". . . enormous waterfalls of the sun" . . . nice image, but sounds like a rationalization to me. Maybe you just don't like the idea of digging through all of your boxes and files and making some sense out of your life. Entering those archives can be pretty daunting.

B: Possibly, but it's also true that I love the loose connections and blurry edges just like they are. You know. Some people get a lot of pleasure out of putting things in order: photo albums-linen closets. Not me. I'm just not interested in dating my eggs, and I don't *mind* shuffling my photographs in drawers. Chronologies are arbitrary anyway, and I prefer more random juxtapositions.

A: You're losing me.

B: Well, think about it. If you put all of your pictures in an album: label them, "John's Wedding," or "Rainforest Trip," or whatever, they will pretty much tell the same story every time. Eventually, they will even come to define the wedding or the trip in a particular way that may or may not be an accurate account of the event.

A: It's better than nothing. At least it can remind you of the way it was.

B: But, if the pictures are mixed up in several drawers and boxes without regard to times or events, when you pull them out, there are wonderful surprises. Juxtapositions! Cherry pies and Hawaiian sunsets, bon voyage bouquets and funeral wreaths, or your face over and over at different ages, but always with that same self-conscious smile.

A: I hadn't thought of it that way.

B: Energy comes from juxtapositions! Energy that comes from rubbing. . . one image against another.

A: You got that off the Bill Moyer's poetry special the other night.

B: But it's true.

A: You're trying to convince yourself that portfolios are not your style. Why don't you take your cue from the Nike ad, and "JUST DO IT." Organize it any way you like. Think about what's important to you. Then, use dividers to separate the topics. . .

B: Like "Comforts of Home" or "Lifelong Learning"?

A: That'll do for starters.

B: Dividers are a little arbitrary, don't you think? Considering that everything is connected to everything else, and besides, what would I put in it? I mean, life is not a series of products, but processes which continue and may or may not leave tracks.

A: There you go again.

(fade to contemplative blue)
LATER

A: How's that portfolio coming along?

B: Haven't started it yet.

A: Why not?

B: It just seems like an awful lot of work if I'm not really going to be using it for anything. When you make a portfolio, you have to ask yourself, "Who's it for?" Obviously, if I were seeking a job overseas, I wouldn't put together the same kind of portfolio as I would to apply for a job in landscape architecture. Besides, if I were looking for a new line of work, which I'm not, I would probably waive the portfolio idea altogether. It's more likely I'd scope the place out, talk to people, learn the language. Sort of like making friends with the place. Then, for the interview, I'd bring in only documents and records of experience relevant to the job I'm after.

A: Still fighting the portfolio concept I see.

B: Oh, not so much. I've started to gather materials for it, but I think I'm going to have to call it a "Personal" Portfolio. I can't imagine anyone else would be interested in its contents.

A: You might be surprised.

B: It's pretty dry. Resumés, transcripts, certificates, kudos, letters of recommendation. . . It's all old business to me. Even *I* can't get interested in it.

A: *You* can put anything you want in it.

B: Okay. Then I choose to put NOTHING in it. It will be a portfolio that begins with nothing. It will include ideas, schemes, travel plans, promises. It'll be based on future events. Now, I can get excited about that.

A: I'll bet you can't *do* that.

B: Do what?

A: Base a portfolio only on events that have not yet happened.

B: Why not?

A: Because tomorrow doesn't exist in the absence of the past which supports it. The whole idea of "future" presupposes that there is a "past," doesn't it? I'll bet you won't be able to put together a portfolio about yourself without bringing in things from your past.

B: I can try.

(fade to tentative amber)
LATER

B: You again. You've come back to congratulate yourself on being right, I suppose.

A: I knew you couldn't do it!

B: Yes, but what you didn't anticipate is that I would really enjoy putting this thing together once I got started.

A: I knew that, too.

B: I'm finding out my life isn't as random as I thought. I do seem to actually have a few underlying organizational principals. I'm starting to see patterns and strands that I hadn't really noticed before. Recurring themes. Seems I actually took the same linguistics class twice. Twenty years apart at different universities. Pretty funny.

A: Well, are you going to show me what you have so far? Isn't that an old Georgia O'Keefe calendar? It makes a great portfolio. And you made pockets for the "artifacts." Looks like you've been playing around with the pictures. Added some poetry, too. Nice.

B: Actually, I've been thinking that my students might like to do a project like this. An adapted version, of course.

A: Now you're talking.

B: I'm even toying with the idea of reorganizing the sections after I retire. You know. Create new juxtapositions, add fresh material.

A: Okay then, what would the new divisions be?

B: Think I'll keep it simple. How about this?
IN   OUT   AROUND   and   THROUGH

A: I don't get it.

B: Oh, never mind.

(fade to comfortable rose)

Notes

Frontispiece: "On Marking the Mind of a Student," by Fran Claggett, was first printed in *Black Birds and Other Birds,* a book of poems by Mary Frances Claggett, published by Taurean Horn Press, 1980.

Chapter One

1. See *Balancing the Hemispheres: Brain Research and the Teaching of Writing,* by Gabriele Lusser Rico and Mary Frances Claggett, University of California, Berkeley, Curriculum Publication No. 14.
2. Gardner, Howard, *Frames of Mind: The Theory of Multiple Intelligences,* Basic Books, Inc., Publishers, New York, 1985, pp. x, xii.
3. Rosenblatt, Louise M., *The Reader, The Text, The Poem,* Southern Illinois University Press, 1978, pp. 24, 25.
4. Ibid., p. 27.
5. Ibid., pp. 23–24.

Chapter Two

The reading scoring guide printed here was developed by the California Reading and Writing Assessment Development team of teachers.

Chapter Three

1. The material on global and secondary writing types is adapted from unpublished documents written by the author for the California Department of Education assessment program. These materials, in somewhat altered form, were used in training and scoring sessions in the 1994 California reading and writing assessment at grades 4, 8, and 10.

"Characteristics of Evaluation as a Writing Type" and the student essay "Love at First Mini-Byte" were published in the California Department of Education *High School Writing Assessment Handbook*, 1993. This handbook was written by the teachers on the California Assessment Development team.

Chapter Four

For a fully developed "angles of vision" lesson on the Icarus poems listed here and other literature study using the angles of vision approach, see *Recasting the Text,* a supplementary high school text from Heinemann-Boynton/Cook, 1996 by Fran Claggett, Louann Reid, and Ruth Vinz.

Chapter Six

1. Roy, Alice. "Review: Critical Literacy, Critical Pedagogy." *College English*, 56 (October 1994):693.

Chapter Seven

1. See the sun-shadow mandala material in *Drawing Your Own Conclusions*, by Fran Claggett and Joan Brown, Heinemann-Boynton/Cook, 1992.
2. For information about the New Standards Project, contact either of the following New Standards offices: National Center on Education and the Economy, 1341 G Street NW, Suite 1020, Washington, DC 20005; or the University of Pittsburgh, Learning Research and Development Center, 3939 O'Hara Street, Pittsburgh, PA 15260.
3. For information about the California Learning Record, write to Mary A. Barr at the Center for Language in Learning, 10610 Quail Canyon Road, El Cajon, CA 92021.

Appendix Four

For an explanation of the stances, see Langer, Judith, "The Process of Understanding Literature," Report Series 2.1, April 1989, Center for the Learning and Teaching of Literature, University at Albany, State University of New York.

Index to Charts, Rubrics, Assignments, and Assessment Strategies

Chapter Four

Chapter Five

Chapter Six

Chapter Seven

Epilogue

Appendices